Thomas Erskine

Advocate for the Character of God

Donald F. Winslow

UNIVERSITY
PRESS OF
AMERICA

Lanham
New York
London

Copyright © 1993 by
University Press of America®, Inc.
4720 Boston Way
Lanham, Maryland 20706

3 Henrietta Street
London WC2E 8LU England

All rights reserved
Printed in the United States of America
British Cataloging in Publication Information Available

Library of Congress Cataloging-in-Publication Data
Winslow, Donald F.
Thomas Erskine : advocate for the character of God /
Donald F. Winslow.
p. cm.
Includes bibliographical references.
1. Erskine, Thomas, 1788–1870. I. Title.
BX4827.E77W56   1992
230'.52'092—dc20   92–24114 CIP

ISBN 0–8191–8836–0 (cloth : alk. paper)
ISBN 0–8191–8837–9 (pbk. : alk. paper)

The paper used in this publication meets the minimum requirements of American National Standard for Information Sciences—Permanence of Paper for Printed Library Materials, ANSI Z39.48–1984.

TABLE OF CONTENTS

Chapter   **Page**

            Abbreviations iv
            Preface v

One	Death and Life 1
Two	The Beginnings of Controversy 13
Three	The Row Heresy 29
Four	The West Country Miracles 43
Five	Biblical Authority 59
Six	The Character of God 73
Seven	The Atonement 85
Eight	Erskine and F. D. Maurice 99

            Appendix 113
            Bibliography 135

ABBREVIATIONS

Baxter..................Introductory Essay to the Saints' Everlasting Rest by the Rev. Richard Baxter.

Election................The Doctrine of Election and its Connection with the General Tenor of Christianity.

Evidence...............Remarks on the Internal Evidence for the Truth of Revealed Religion.

Ewing..................Present-Day Papers on Prominent Questions in Theology, Third Series.

Faith....................An Essay on Faith.

Freeness...............The Unconditional Freeness of the Gospel.

Gambold...............The Works of John Gambold, A.M., with an Introductory Essay, by Thomas Erskine, Esq., Advocate.

Gifts....................The Gifts of the Spirit.

Hanna..................Letters of Thomas Erskine of Linlathen.

Lady....................Extracts of Letters to a Christian Friend by a Lady, with an Introductory Essay by Thomas Erskine.

Rutherford............Letters of the Rev. Samuel Rutherford ... With an Introductory Essay by Thomas Erskine.

Serpent.................The Brazen Serpent, or Life Coming Through Death.

Sp. Order..............The Spiritual Order and Other Papers.

PREFACE

In the winter of 1838 Thomas Carlyle wrote to his younger brother, John, asking him: "Did you ever see Thomas Erskine, the Scotch saint? I have seen him several times lately, and like him as one would a draught of sweet rustic mead, served in cut glasses [on] a silver tray; one of the gentlest, kindliest, best bred of men."[1] Equally fond of him was Carlyle's wife, Jane, who playfully dubbed Erskine "St. Thomas." When, nearly 30 years later, Carlyle was to be installed as [Honorary] Rector of the University of Edinburgh, he declined offers of lodging from several others so that he might stay with the gentle Erskine (and, as his wife observed, so that he might sleep far from the sound of the railway whistles!).[2] On the same occasion as Carlyle's installation, Erskine was to receive an LL.D. from the University, concerning which honor the Edinburgh correspondent of a London Journal wrote: "If intelligent goodness ever entitled anyone to the degree of LL.D., [Erskine] certainly deserves it."[3] In a letter to T.R. Matthews, Erskine wrote, with characteristic modesty: "I believe that the fact of Carlyle being my guest whilst he was in Edinburgh for the purposes of being installed as Lord Rector of the University was the chief reason of my being honoured with the LL.D. degree." And he added, whimsically, "Of course nobody calls me Dr., except for fun."[4])

It is difficult to believe that a man whose intelligence and goodness made such a profound impression on so many of his friends was himself in the 1820s and 1830s the center of a bitter theological controversy, a man whose published works elicited virulent attacks, and a man who was perceived by the ruling ecclesial establishment to be the enemy of biblical truth and confessional orthodoxy. "Being a lay theologian, and not an ordained minister," Henry Henderson wrote toward the end of the century, "[Erskine] was answerable neither to court nor to council ... Ordinary ecclesiastics therefore could afford to ignore him."[5] The evidence, however, gives clear indication that Erskine was not ignored, for "ordinary" clergymen, as well as some "extraordinary" ones, kept Scottish publishing houses busily printing books, pamphlets, letters, and reviews which not only vilified Erskine's theological views but the holder of them as well. But if Erskine the layman was beyond the machinery of the ecclesiastical courts, the "full wrath" of these courts, as Drummond and Bulloch have pointed out, did fall upon his "clerical sympathizers."[6] Chief among these were two men deeply influenced by Erskine, John McLeod Campbell and Frederick Denison Maurice; the former, minister of the church in Row (Rhu), was deposed by a Church of Scotland synod in 1831, and the latter expelled from his professorship at King's College, University of London—both of them for views easily traceable to Erskine's influence, views which the Scottish Synod of Glasgow and Ayr and the Anglican King's College Council condemned as clearly and unambiguously heretical. Yet, if this *odium theologicum* had its dramatic aspect, Erskine's quietly persuasive personality appears to have had a more enduring effect upon those who, like Carlyle, knew him well. Maurice himself spoke of Erskine as "so gentle and truthful and loving; the best man I think I ever knew,"[7] and a friend of Erskine in later years, Alexander Ewing (Episcopal Bishop of Argyll and the Isles whom Erskine often addressed affectionately as *Vescovo carissimo*), admired him immensely, published many of his letters as well as extracts and condensations of his writings, and even saw to their translation into French and Italian (for the edification, one supposes, of the Papists!).[8] "Should anyone attempt to write the *life* of Mr. Erskine," wrote Ewing, "the difficulty must ever present itself to him that what he has to depict is spirit and not matter, that he has to convey light, to represent sound—an almost insuperable difficulty."[9] A further difficulty is represented by the fact that "Scotland has never given Erskine the attention he deserved and his books now are almost unattainable."[10] Yet many historians of nineteenth-century religious thought (by no means all of them Scottish) have testified to Erskine's importance, albeit such testimony has more often than not been confined to just a few pages. Otto Pfleiderer, for instance, made the oft-quoted claim that the writings of Erskine and Campbell were the "best contribution to dogmatics which British theology made in the [19th] century" and that it was Erskine who, "by his own independent study of the Bible, arrived at the conviction that the orthodox representation of the Gospel did not properly represent its real and scriptural nature."[11] Others have said much the same, among them Robert Franks, who saw Erskine as "instrumental in the regeneration of British theology,"[12] and Vernon Storr, who observed that, while Erskine "did not directly attack the traditional theology of his Church, yet the result of his work was to bring about a reinterpretation of the current orthodox doctrine."[13] John Tulloch's assessment is similar: [W]hile Erskine never personally attacked the dogmas of the church, he yet, in all his writings, tended quietly to subvert them."[14] Robert Story, whose father was intimately involved in the controversies arising out of Erskine's views, saw Erskine as the author of a "freer and deeper theology," and thus a "pioneer" of a movement "which has ultimately broken the gloomy domination of the theology that has been so cramped in its growth by the shackles of Westminster that its continued influence would have, sooner or later, extinguished the [country's] spiritual and intellectual liberty."[15] And Julia Wedgwood, whose writings deserve to be better known, admitting that Erskine's views were not only startlingly unfamiliar but close to actual heresy, nevertheless characterized him as the prime "agent" by which the "hard Calvinism" of his day was "subsequently put to rest."[16] The strongly articulated opinions of both his critics and his supporters, then, and the more charitable and appreciative assessments of later generations, all portray Erskine as a man whose specifically theological significance—both within the context of his own century as well as for our own age—needs to be rescued from near oblivion. Too, Erskine's writings (which are indeed "almost unattainable") are a vigorous, original, and lively contribution to the development of liberal thought. The man was, happily, not without his faults nor his writings without their inconsistencies and (sometimes) egregious errors, but faults and errors, in Erskine's case, add a spicy richness to a theological perspective from which anyone concerned with the pursuit of Christian truth can greatly benefit. It is to this end that this present volume is dedicated.

Unfortunately, I was unable, prior to the completion of my work, to obtain a copy of Nicholas R. Needham's excellent study, *Thomas Erskine of Linlathen: His Life and Theology 1788-1837* (Edinburgh: Rutherford House Books, 1990). I heartily commend this book to my readers.

All quotations from Erskine's writings are from the edition indicated in the Bibliography. The only editing of these quotations has been the removal of occasional commas so as to render the meaning more clearly and the flow of the sentences less choppy. Erskine, it seems, was as profligate with commas as his near contemporary Sydney Smith was parsimonious.

To the competent and always helpful staffs of the British Library in London, the Bodleian Library in Oxford, St. Deiniol's Library in Hawarden, The National Library of Scotland, the University of Edinburgh Library, and the New College Library, a word of extreme gratitude. And, to the Conant fund (of the Board for Theological Education) and the Theological Writer's Fund (of the Episcopal Divinity School) my thanks for their generous grants without which I would have been unable to pursue my travels and research.

Many others—too numerous to mention—have assisted me with their comments, criticisms, and suggestions. They know who they are, but they may never know how truly I have appreciated their support.

Notes to Preface

[1] Thomas Carlyle, *Letters of Thomas Carlyle to his Youngest Sister*, Edited with an Introductory Essay by Charles Townsend Copeland (London, 1899), p. 101.

[2] Fred Kaplan, *Thomas Carlyle: A Biography* (Ithaca, 1983), p. 465 and Shepherd and Williamson (ed.), *Memoirs of the Life and Writings of Thomas Carlyle, with Personal Reminiscences, &c.* (London, 1881), Vol. 2, p. 200.

[3] Shepherd & Williamson, *op. cit.*, Vol. 2, p. 212.

[4] Hanna, p. 378, and quoted by W. H. Wylie, *Thomas Carlyle: The Man and his Books* (London, 1881), p. 276.

[5] H. F. Henderson (ed.), *Erskine of Linlathen: Selections and Biography* (Edinburgh and London, 1899), p. 87.

[6] Drummond and Bulloch, *The Scottish Church 1688-1843* (Edinburgh, 1973), p. 199.

[7] F. Maurice, *The Life of Frederick Denison Maurice* (New York, 1884), Vol. 1, p. 533.

[8] The extent of Erskine's theological influence on Ewing can be seen in the latter's *An Address to the Younger Clergy and Laity on the Present State of Religion* (London, 1865) in which all the leading ideas are close to being pure Erskine.

[9] Alexander Ewing, *Present-Day Papers on Prominent Questions in Theology*, Third Series (London, 1878), Part 1, p. 12. Ewing's commentary upon visiting with Erskine is similar to that of many others: "It is always a great gain to be with him. I learn more from his conversations than from all the books I read. His looks and life of love are better than a thousand homilies." (Quoted by Hanna [p. 405, n. 1] from *Memoir of Bishop Ewing*.)

[10] Drummond & Bulloch, *op. cit.*, p. 199. An anonymous reviewer of Hanna's *Letters of Thomas Erskine* (Vol. 2) makes this wistful comment: "[W]e will not disguise our deliberate opinion that the representatives and friends of this great inaugurator of the Third Scotch Reformation would have better provided for the Catholic canonisation of [Erskine's] name, and would have better served the cause of spiritual progress, if they had entrusted Dr. Hanna with the responsibilities of a genuine biography, instead of restricting him to the comparatively mechanical task of an editor." *The Spectator*, Dec. 29, 1877, p. 1661.

[11] Otto Pfleiderer, *The Development of Theology in Germany since Kant and its Progress in Great Britain since 1825* (London, 1890), pp. 378 and 382.

[12] Robert S. Franks, *The Work of Christ* (London, 1962), p. 655

[13] V. F. Storr, *The Development of English Theology in the Nineteenth Century, 1800-1860* (London, 1913), p. 355. To refer to the Church of Scotland as *his* church is an error in as much as Erskine was in fact an Episcopalian, albeit never comfortable within the confines of any one denominational boundary.

[14] John Tulloch, *Movements of Religious Thought in Britain during the Nineteenth Century* (New York, 1971), p. 132.

[15] R. H. Story, *The Apostolic Ministry in the Scottish Church* (Edinburgh & London, 1897), pp. 307-308.

[16] Julia Wedgwood, "Thomas Erskine of Linlathen," in *Nineteenth Century Teachers and Other Essays* (London, 1909), p. 165.

CHAPTER ONE: DEATH AND LIFE

"I am now in my eightieth year," wrote Erskine to his friend John Campbell Shairp. "It is a wonderful thing to discover that I am so old. I seem all at once to have made a start forward without passing through the intermediate stages. I know, however, that I am at the boundaries of the unseen world, and that I must soon enter that untried state ... "[1] Two and a half years later, in March of 1879, Erskine did approach the boundaries of that untried state and, a few days before he died, his attending physician and friend, Dr. John Brown, wrote this account to Shairp:

> God only knows what an awful thing it is to be so near Heaven as I am when near him. He is past all fear and darkness. He is falling asleep, as a child in its mother's bosom ... and speaks out his dreams such utterances of love and tender and subtle thought; bits of his essential self, the perfected flower of a life with God.[2]

Such sentiments regarding Erskine are so numerous and come from so wide a variety of persons that they cannot be dismissed simply as rhetorical hyperbole. Arthur Penrhyn Stanley, for instance, was introduced by Shairp to Erskine and later wrote that to hold brief converse with him was "to have one's conversation in heaven."[3] Shairp it was who wrote a touching memorial to Erskine which appeared in *The Scotsman* of 31 March 1870, a memorial which was later considerably expanded in a letter of "Reminiscences" and published by William Hanna. In recalling his several visits to Erskine at the latter's estate in Linlathen, Shairp observed: "It used to be a strange feeling to walk about the place with him, wearing as he did, the guise of the Scottish Laird, while all the while his inner spirit, you felt, was breathing the atmosphere of St. John." And when left to himself, Shairp went on to say, Erskine was "a man absorbed by the thought of God," a man for whom, as with Jacob Boehme, the "heart of God" was as much his element as water to the fish or air to the bird (Hanna, p. 528).

It would appear, then, that Erskine lived constantly on the boundaries of the unseen world and that the "untried state" to which death was the gateway was already proleptically familiar to him throughout his lifetime. Indeed, death was for Erskine not so much the entrance into what he often referred to as the "spiritual world" as it was the transition into a fuller awareness of that spiritual world already known to us through the Gospel. God is not on the other side of the boundary between the temporal and the eternal; rather, God is constantly with us and in us, instructing us, communicating the "divine nature" to us, cajoling us, persuading us, luring us into a lively and living recognition of that love which has no limits, a love whose essential characteristic is that it is "inextinguishable" (Sp. Order, p. 59).

Two biblical texts Erskine was never weary of quoting: "For I am not ashamed of the Gospel of Christ: for it is the power of God unto salvation" (Rom. 1.16) and [T]his is eternal life, that they might know thee, the only true God, and Jesus Christ, whom thou has sent" (John 17.3). The *present* power of the Gospel and the *present* knowledge of God made it impossible for Erskine to conceive of salvation as the reward for the faithful *after* they die and "go to heaven." Erskine understood salvation in a completely different (and more biblical) way. Salvation is a process graciously begun in creation and is therefore within the reach of all people, now. While some of Erskine's contemporaries averred that eternal life was that future state into which the "elect" are to be conducted, Erskine himself experienced eternal life as a present disposition to and appropriation of the Good News of God in Jesus Christ.[4] Death, then, is neither the end of this life nor the beginning of a radically new state of being. Nor is death the "enemy," for in Christ Jesus the enemy has been defeated. The power of the enemy may yet abound, but the victory has in principle been accomplished. We need not therefore be afraid.

Thomas Erskine was born in October of 1788, and from the time of his earliest years, death was an ever-present reality, so much so that, even as a youngster, he may have perceived it as the one, single, relentless enemy. His father, David Erskine, died in Naples (where he had gone for his health)[5] in 1791 when Thomas was not yet three years of age. (Six months later, Thomas' younger sister was born and named David—most often called Davie—after her now dead father.) Thomas' two older brothers had died previously, William in 1784 and John in 1789, while his older sister Ann died in 1804 when she was but fifteen years old and Thomas sixteen. A fourth child of David and Anne Erskine, James, grew to maturity, served briefly as a captain in the army before retiring in 1811 to Linlathen (originally "Lumlaythum"), the estate in Forfarshire near Dundee which his father had purchased some years earlier. But death still stalked the Erskines. James and his wife Katherine had four children, all of whom died within a few days of their birth. And James himself died in 1816 at the age of twenty-eight. Many years later , Erskine wrote of his brother James: "I think my brother was the most remarkable man I ever knew ... He was only a year older than myself, and I venerated him from my infancy ... That upper world must be a wonderful meeting-place—meeting in God" (Hanna, p. 13). What Thomas wrote just a few weeks after his brother's death is, understandably, more poignant: "[My] heart is stunned; I have lost a Christian friend, a spiritual guide. But thanks be to God, I can look to the Good Shepherd, and can trust Him for the supply of all my wants, for remission of sins, and for renewal of heart, and for faith that I may see His wise love in all his dispensations towards me. Many new duties are indeed imposed upon me, and I beg the prayers of my friends for grace to discharge them to the glory of the Imposer" (Hanna, p. 15).

Chief of these many new duties was the administration of the estate at Linlathen, a task which meant that Erskine could no longer pursue a promising career as an advocate, a career in which his paternal grandfather, John Erskine (the author of *Institutes of the Law of Scotland*), had so distinguished himself. Haunted at the time by the premature death of so many of his relatives (including that of his

CHAPTER ONE: DEATH AND LIFE

cousin Patrick Stirling in 1816), and struggling to discern the hand (dispensation or imposition?) of a loving God in such events, Erskine wrote a farewell essay to his colleagues at the Bar which, although it was not to be published until some years later and in an entirely different context, [6] demonstrated that even as a young man, without any formal religious training, he was at heart a theologian or, we might say, an "advocate" for the "character of God." This early essay, originally entitled "Salvation," was an attempt on Erskine's part to discern the relationship between God's justice and God's mercy and to give utterance to his not yet fully developed understanding of salvation. Much of what Erskine wrote in it would later be revised or corrected, but several of the underlying themes of the Essay reappear frequently in his subsequent writings. One can see in this little work Erskine's growing perception of God's purpose for creation and his intense experience of God's redemptive benevolence, in spite of the cruel phenomenon of death—a perception and an experience which from this time onwards become the subject and object of both his written works and his letters and conversations. Yet such views were also to bring him into close conflict with many of the leading theologians of the day, especially those for whom death was the "wages of sin" and "everlasting punishment" the surest testimony to God's unswerving righteousness.

These formative elements in Erskine's theological outlook found palpable expression in his life as he found himself increasingly able to give comfort to others who were mourning the death of loved ones or who were themselves dying. His letters to such persons, to friends and relatives as well as to strangers, are a remarkable witness to Erskine's profound conviction in respect to God's compassion; the letters never fall into that strained and formalistic style which mark so many letters of consolation of the nineteenth century. Grief is never ridiculed as a want of trust in God, and trust in God is never offered as a pietistic sop for grief. Yet God can be trusted, and grief, for all its apparent finality, is not the last word.

Such comfort was communicated not only by letter; Erskine also went personally (often at someone else's request) to visit the afflicted, seeking always to arouse in them an awareness of God's presence and abiding love. His readiness to travel, often many miles, to be with those who were dying has elicited from one writer the wry comment that Erskine had a "penchant for death-bed visits," and that, after being present at the death of his Cousin Patrick, "death-beds became his specialty."[7] Bishop Ewing relates a story, originally told him by a certain Lady Matilda Maxwell of Polloc (Ewing, iv, pp. 17-19), of the time when Erskine was persuaded to visit a farmer who, although he was deathly ill, refused to admit that he was sick, so afraid was he to die. Upon being ushered into the sick man's room, Erskine immediately began speaking of death and of the need to be prepared for it. "What do *you* know of death?" was the farmer's bitter retort. This led Erskine to retreat from the topic and to introduce "country matters" into the conversation—planting, the soil, the weather, and the like. To this the farmer responded happily, and soon he and Erskine were talking like old friends. Sensing that he had won the farmer's trust, Erskine again broached the subject of death: "I cannot leave you without telling you that you are indeed going to die. Are you prepared?" "I'm sure you mean well, Sir," was the reply, "but how can I prepare? What can I do?" "Well, let me ask you this: now that we are friends, and now that you are embarking upon a journey, would you like me to go with you?" The farmer looked puzzled. "How can that be?" he asked. "Apart from whether or not it *can* be," replied Erskine, "would you still like me to go with you?" "Yes, I would. Definitely. You seem to be the kind of friend that wouldn't let anything bad happen to me." "I am glad that you trust me. Yet I assure you that you can trust God even more, for God is not only the wonderful destination of your journey but also your companion on the way." Struck by the sincerity of Erskine's faith, the farmer is said to have exchanged his earlier fear and anger for a happy confidence. His death was calm and peaceful.

"I feel it always to be a great privilege," wrote Erskine, "to be with the dying, and I have enjoyed this privilege" (Hanna, p. 81). And in the exercise of this "privilege," Erskine developed a capacity to communicate a comfort and assurance which sprang from deep theological roots. God's enduring friendship for the whole of the human race was a central and abiding theme of Erskine's thought, a theme articulated in conscious contradistinction to the view that God, even more than death, was the enemy, the one whose anger and wrath somehow needed to be propitiated, whose favor needed to be earned, and whose salvific mercy was limited to the "elect." The positive dimensions of Erskine's early theological views are to be found in the very first of his published works (1820), a slim volume entitled, *Remarks on the Internal Evidence for the Truth of Revealed Religion*. It is here that he gives voice to his perception of the "history" of God's dealing with humankind: it is a history, he says, which "gives peace to the conscience ... dispels the terrors of guilt ... [and] inspires a pure and elevated and joyful hope for eternity" (Evidence, p. 14). The Bible, he goes on to say, "presents a history of wondrous love in order to excite gratitude; of high and holy worth, to attract veneration and esteem. It presents a view of danger, to produce alarm; of refuge, to confer peace and joy; and of eternal glory, to animate hope" (Evidence, p. 40).

Such a message, rare given the theological tenor of the day, found many grateful adherents. In the next few years the book went through nine editions and was translated into French and German as well. One eulogistic response came from Erskine's friend Alexandre Vinet:

> J'ai lu en entier, avec un plaisir bien pur, le livre d'Erskine; je compte bien le relire ... Si je ne haïssais par principe ces expressions: Je suis d'Apollos et de Céphas, je me laisserais aller volontier à dire: Je suis d'Erskine (Hanna, p. 27).

CHAPTER ONE: DEATH AND LIFE

Even the *Edinburgh Christian Instructor*, "prompt as that organ of the Evangelical party in Scotland was to detect the slightest deviation from Calivinistic theology" (Hanna, p. 22), commended the book to the reading public with high praises, as did the more liberal *Edinburgh Review*.[8] There is in fact little to criticize in this early work, although one reviewer observed that, while the book "exhibits the primary evidence in support of Revealed Religion with much force, feeling, and clearness," what Erskine has written would have been more effective "if the ground on which an appeal to the internal evidence is rested had been more clearly defined."[9] What is clear, however, is that Erskine's whole approach to the question of "evidence" was unusual, given the many books published in the eighteenth and nineteenth century on that popular topic (the best known of which is William Paley's *View of the Evidences of Christianity*, published in 1794). Soame Jenyns, for instance, had published in 1776 a little book with a title surprisingly similar to Erskine's: *A View of the Internal Evidence of the Christian Religion*. He introduces his treatise with the observation that, while prophesy and miracles are often appealed to in order to substantiate the claims of Christianity, "internal evidence ... seems to carry with it the greatest degree of conviction [and has never been given] the attention it deserves."[10] There is no indication that Erskine ever read Jenyns' book, but had he done so he would have found it superficial in the extreme, given his own understanding of what is meant by *internal* evidence. Jenyns was content merely to assert that the New Testament's "system of religion" was entirely new and that its "system of ethics" was higher than any known, both of which facts point unerringly to the divine origin of the New Testament, and hence of Christianity! John Smyth, who was to become a virulent critic of Erskine's views on universal forgiveness, did not do much better. Some eighteen years after the publication of Erksine's *Evidence*, he wrote an article entitled "Internal Evidence of Christianity." Smyth's was a more detailed and thorough study than Jenyns' but shared his historical and theological naïveté as well as his biblical fideism. His thesis was that the "purity" of scripture, the "sublimity" of scriptural doctrines, and the "harmony and consistency" of scripture principles all point to the absolute truth of Christianity. An indication of the kind of argumentation found in this book is Smyth's response to the alleged contradictions in the New Testament (e.g., between the genealogies in Matthew and Luke). He waves this difficulty away with the bland assertion: "[W]e affirm that the truth of the Christian revelation may be fearlessly committed to the harmony of consistency of its statements of doctrine and duty, provided the subject be examined with humility, assiduity, and prayerful dependence on the illumination of the Spirit of God."[11] There is no indication that Erskine read this book either!

Erskine must have been aware that his views were radically different from those who wrote on the same subject; aware, too, that what he had written was not in the mainstream of Westminster orthodoxy, although he wrote with no specific opponent in mind. His concern, rather, was to invite his reader into a deeper knowledge of and greater appreciation for the Bible as a source of "Divine knowledge." More than Creeds and Confessions, which tend to be doctrinally limited or limiting, the Bible, in its narration of God's actions within human history, "addresses the learned and the unlearned, and savage and the civilized, the decent and the profligate" in such a way as to reveal those actions to be consonant with God's character and purpose and at the same time capable of exercising a direct influence on the human character: "The great argument for the truth of Christianity lies in the sanctifying influence of its doctrines; and, alas! the great argument against it lies in the unsanctified lives of its professors" (Evidence, p. 76). And just as God's love knows no limits, so too the potential influence of that love knows no limits: the Gospel message is "amply sufficient for the most guilty [person]; and it is fitted to implant in the vilest heart which will receive it the principles of true penitence and true gratitude, of ardent attachment to the holy character of God, and of cordial devotion to [God's] will" (p. 92). Creeds and Confessions, arising as they do out of prejudiced points of view, tend to *defend* Christianity; the Bible, however, *teaches* it. And the "radical principle" which the Bible teaches is, quite specifically, the love of God.

Erskine's understanding of the authority of the Bible and of the fallibility of human speculation will be discussed in greater detail subsequently; it is important at this time, however, to say that, if this first work of his was well received,[12] and led many of his readers to think of him as a theological author of exceptional promise, in this book (as we shall see) there are also to be found the seeds of those views which were to provoke that acrimonious controversy to which I have already referred. Yet Erskine had no intent—at least until he became aware of the attacks being made upon him—of being either novel or controversial. Indeed he ends his book with an almost apologetic and certainly irenic caveat: "There is nothing new in this cursory sketch of Christian doctrines. Indeed, I should conceive a proof of novelty as tantamount to a proof of error" (p. 138).

Nor was there anything radically new or revolutionary in the next work of Erskine's, a short essay published in 1822 which served originally as an introduction to an edition of the works of John Gambold (1711-1771). Yet the *tone* of the essay, if not its specific theological precepts, may have struck many of its readers as novel since, rather than succumbing to the dour pessimism of so much of Scottish Calvinism, it was a clear articulation of that joy which Erskine associated with one's relationship to God. Our several relationships, he wrote, such as those to one's family or to one's vocation or profession, may produce happiness or despair; we have no ultimate power, however, to change the nature or duration of such relationships or the circumstances in which they exist. But there is one "grand and important relationship," the root of the others, and this is our relationship with our Creator God. And it is here, for Erskine, that we discover that it is God alone who can change our circumstances so that our secondary or inferior relationships, if tragic, will not overwhelm us and, if happy, will not lead us to neglect the One who is the source of our genuine joy. We can know this joy and appropriate it personally because, in Christ Jesus, our offenses have been forgiven and the gates to that arena in which dwells God's own family have been thrown open, and we have been invited to speak of God as "Father," and to lean on God as a "faithful and tender friend" (Gambold, p. xi). It is, to use Erskine's own secular analogy, as if an unconditional amnesty had been proclaimed and trustworthy pledges of the grantor of it given and our ultimate safety surely guaranteed. Of course, if one does not trust or believe in the grantor, the amnesty will be no more useful (radically to change the metaphor!) than telling a blind person that the color of the bedroom furniture has been changed. God has invited us to open our eyes and to discover that the furniture of our environment has in fact been changed; no longer are we surrounded by objects of terror and despair; our dwelling place has been changed from "earth" to "heaven," the very heaven of which God can say to us, "Come up here," precisely because God has, in the person of Jesus Christ, united himself to us. Herein lies our joy, a joy to be possessed not only by "advanced Christians" but by those who believe themselves most unworthy of God's love. Joy, in a word, "is the first fruit of the Gospel of Christ" (p. xxi; cf. Gal. 5:22).

Erskine concluded this happy essay with the observation that the chief value of Gambold's writings lay in the fact that they were not "fatally and foolishly' given to "speculative discussion," since "metaphysicians and poets [albeit Gambold was a poet!] are very apt to convert the gospel into an ingenious argument [or] a beautiful dream." Gambold's, however, was an *affective* theology, the chief value of which was that if offered a "permanent profit" rather than a "passing pleasure," and that its power lay in its ability to produce "feeling and action" (pp. xxiv-xxv). One cannot but wonder whether it was Erskine's deep affection for Gambold's writings that produced in his own writings a similar, or perhaps even stronger, affective quality, a quality which was, in his later years, to become increasingly evident.

The year 1822 saw yet another publication from Erskine's hand, this one a work entitled, *An Essay on Faith*. Had Erskine been influenced by contemporary German thought, or had he written the Essay in the twentieth century, it might have been called: *The Phenomenology of Believing: a Disclaimer*, for in it there is continuing evidence of Erskine's abiding dissatisfaction with "scholastic metaphysics," in this case with the "metaphysical labyrinth" in which various modes of believing are endlessly predicated and tiresomely analyzed. Erskine's purpose in the Essay was to draw attention from the *act* of believing and direct it to the *object* of belief, to move our concern, that is, from the "how" of believing to the "what it is" we believe or the "who is it in whom" we believe (Faith, pp. 17 & 114). The principle behind this stated purpose can be seen in Erskine's assertion that belief, in and of itself, is an abstract phenomenon which leads to nothing, whereas that belief which genuinely contemplates the gospel of Jesus Christ or the revealed character of God, such a belief can produce a dramatic change in the believer. People may speak, for instance, or write 'orthodoxly" without either understanding or acting upon those doctrines which are professed. But where, asks Erskine, is the meaning of the Gospel for such persons? We are not called to believe in or have faith in (the two terms are mostly synonymous for Erskine) a specific doctrine so as to prove our willingness to submit to some abstract notion of God's authority; we are called to believe, rather, so that we may be "influenced" by the object of our belief (p. 25). To believe, for instance, that "God so loved the world ..." is a vain thing unless an *impression* is made on us that, even as we are now perishing, the true reality is that we have by God's graciousness been delivered. This, for Erskine, as in his Introductory Essay to Gambold's works, can lead to nothing less than joy (p. 38). And this joy makes a palpable difference; by it our characters are conformed to the image of God who is made known to us in the gospel, since "the perfections of our characters will depend on the perfection of the impressions which we receive from the gospel" (p. 41). "Base and polluted beings" that we are, God has addressed us directly, perhaps first as selfish persons who gladly respond to the instinct of self-preservation; subsequently, however, as our moral power develops and as the Spirit increasingly assists us in discerning the truth, to that joy which is born of a grateful delight in God, a God who is for us, and therefore to a love which will grow more and more disinterested. And then "the glory of God will be contemplated with a rapture unmixed with selfish thoughts" (p. 47).

The truths of revelation are addressed, Erskine believed, to our given capacity to receive them and, no matter how depraved we might be, ultimately to our God-given capacity to respond. They are addressed, that is, to our already existing moral principles and natural feelings. "A poor, ignorant, naked savage, who knows and feels ... that he is a sinner, that God hates sin yet has mercy on the sinner, knows and believes more of the Gospel than the most acute and most orthodox theologian whose heart has never been touched by the love of God" (p. 67). Erskine was confident that there is, in each of us, something that can respond to the Gospel. There is in each of us, therefore, the potential for being conformed to God's image: "[T]he most hardened sinner has yet some conscience left" (p. 79). Even to that sinner, as to all of us, God has been presented, clothed in our human nature, walking and conversing in our company, fulfilling all the offices and suffering all the sorrows of life so that we might be relieved of the sense of terror and alienation and be gifted with a "respectful confidence and intimacy." God has given, that is, "tangible form to the high attributes of deity." God has become our true "dwelling place" (p. 82). This is the object of our belief, the object by which "our affections are excited," for implicit in it is the proclamation that God's pardon is an act of the past, already wrought in Christ's death and resurrection. Those who believe, then, are gradually sanctified by the object of their belief; they are not, mind you, by virtue of their belief gradually pardoned! Given the persistence of our sinfulness, as countered by the insistence of God's forgiving benevolence, we are able, all of us, to walk together with a graceful combination of humility and confidence.

Erskine's *An Essay on Faith* was also well received; subsequent editions were forthcoming and soon a French translation. The only serious negative critique of the book came, some years later (in 1836), from an unlikely source: John Henry Newman. Newman wrote a prolonged Tract attacking both it and Erskine's *Internal Evidence*. Perhaps too gratuitously he referred to Erskine as "an author, concerning whom personally I have no wish to use one harsh word, not doubting that he is better than his own doctrine, and is only the organ, eloquent and ingenious, of unfolding a theory which it has been his unhappiness to mistake for the Catholic faith revealed in the Gospel."[13] It is clear from reading Newman's Tract that his growing "Catholic" proclivities prevented him from understanding what Erskine was saying in *An Essay on Faith*, for his major criticism was that the author had fallen into the trap of "rationalism," and by doing so had become forgetful of God's power, raising human knowledge up as the final arbiter of divine revelation. Erskine's views were in fact, as Newman perceived them, "unlawful and presumptuous," setting the moral significance of a given doctrine above its capacity to enshrine a "mystery." Happy to wave doctrinal shibboleths, Newman concluded by pillorying Erskine's views as not only rationalistic but as tending also (alas!) toward universalism; and, if not in actual contradiction to the Athanasian Creed, probably closer to the errors of Sabellianism or Socianism!

Apart from Newman's misdirected attack, Erskine's early theological writings elicited no harsh retorts and raised no suspicions as to his "orthodoxy."[14] And yet, as I have already indicated, intimations of those views which would subsequently cause such a stir were indeed present in the writings of 1820 and 1822. One can see in these works, for instance, a strong dislike for "speculative" theology and for "metaphysical" argumentation—both of these were, for Erskine, alien to the mode and style of the biblical testimony. There are also to be found strong hints of Erskine's concern that an over-cautious appeal to "orthodoxy" may result in exchanging one's loyalty to and experience of the living God for a slavish adherence to Creed or Confession. Too, Erskine's emphasis on God's unending compassion would later draw accusations that he underplayed God's righteous wrath and therefore, by belittling the reality of sin, was dangerously close to, if not an actual advocate of, antinomianism. And, finally, the "confidence" with which Erskine spoke of God's relationship to all of humankind not only detracted from the received "Doctrine of Election" as understood in the Church of Scotland, but also came perilously close to the "novel and antiscriptural Doctrine of Assurance."

During these years, however, Erskine had no concern for controversy. In September of 1821, his youngest sister David was married to James Paterson and, upon Erskine's request, the young couple took up residence at Linlathen, affording him, the following August, to make a much longed-for extended visit to the Continent. It was to be a sojourn of three year's duration. His esteem for John Gambold was enhanced by a visit to Herrnhut, the "metropolis of Moravianism." He wrote often and ecstatically of the great works of art he was privileged to see, especially in Dresden, Florence, and Rome. "God," he observed simply, "is the source of beauty" (Hanna, p. 50). He rejoiced in new friendships but confessed his lack of fluency in European languages: "My want of German is a great want, and a great stupidity moreover, which I am now endeavoring to correct as fast as I can" (Hanna, p. 31). He reflected, while abroad, on the differences between Arminianism and Calvinism and once wrote briefly in favor of the doctrine of predestination, even if it was not to be derived directly from the Bible (a view he was later to dismiss). But most of all, Erskine's trip abroad was a pilgrimage with and among Christian friends in whose company he indulged happily in "Christian conversation" and "Christian intercourse." Even when alone, Erskine's thoughts seldom strayed from his characteristic preoccupation with religious concerns: "I have been in absolute solitude for three weeks ... But I am very comfortable and happy when I can keep near God; and solitude is not adverse to that, though, and at the same time, it will not produce it ... The constant sense of the Divine presence is the important thing and the delightful thing, and, at the same time, wonderful to say, it is the great difficulty ..." (Hanna, p. 41).

The "delight" would remain with Erskine all his life, as indeed would also the "difficulty." Both as resident "Laird of Linlathen" and as frequent traveller abroad, his capacity for theological reflection matured. Not by nature argumentative, he sought always to speak the truth, at whatever risk, as he had been given to perceive it, and, as his theological sensitivities developed, he learned not to shy away from vigorously questioning those views which he found to be antithetical to the biblical revelation of God's love, but never did he personally attack the holders of such views. (The same cannot be said for many of his opponents!)

One American observer, the peripatetic Moncure Daniel Conway, that inveterate name-dropper, said of Erskine that "he wrote much on [religion] but lost his Calvinism by going to study in Germany. He was now not much in favor because of his scepticism."[15] That Erskine "lost his Calvinism" is certainly true, although whether it was as a result of his going to Germany may not be so. But that Erskine at some time turned "sceptic" is totally unsupported by the evidence. The religious sensitivities which were so uniquely his because of his early experience with death remained throughout his life, even to that time in his eightieth year when he articulated his surprise at having grown so old. And Shairp, as we have seen, marvelled in turn that the quality of that long life was so enriched by its being a life that was lived so constantly and so intimately in the presence of God. Little can Shairp have known that he was quoting the man who accused Erskine of so many doctrinal errors when he took John Henry Newman's description of St. John in his old age as applicable to Erskine:

> He was as a man moving his goods into a far country, who at intervals and by portions sends them before him, till his present abode is well nigh unfurnished. He had sent forward his friends on their journey, while he himself stayed behind, that there might be those in heaven to have thoughts of him, to look out for him, and receive him when the Lord should call (Hanna, p. 536).

Upon Erskine's return from Europe, there were many years yet to be traversed before he reached that "far country," many "delights" and many "difficulties" to be experienced before he would arrive at the "boundaries of that unseen world." The most pressing of these difficulties would be the turmoil aroused by the next several of his published works, as well as by the "guilt by association" laid upon him by virtue of his support of and friendship with the Rev. John McLeod Campbell of Row. One wonders if Shairp had these bitter controversies in mind when, in his *Essay on Keble*, he wrote:

> Polemics by themselves are dreary work. They do not touch the springs of young hearts. But he who, in the midst of any line of thought, unlocks a fountain of genuine poetry, does more to harmonise it, and win for it a way to [our] affections, than he who writes a hundred volumes, however able, of controversy.[16]

Yet, in spite of the bitterness of the controversies that were to evolve, Erskine, by the increasingly focused nature of his views, bequeathed to British theology a legacy the influence of which is still, however unconsciously, felt today. As one author has observed: "[T]he liberation of the mind from hard, unhappy views of Divine truth [has] been perhaps more directly due to the teaching and personal character of Thomas Erskine than to any other source of influence that can be named."[17]

Notes to Chapter One

[1] W.A. Knight, *Principal Shairp and His Friends* (London, 1888), pp. 213-4.

[2] *Ibid.*, p. 222.

[3] R.E. Prothero, *The Life and Correspondence of Arthur Penrhyn Stanley* (New York, 1894) Vol. 2, p. 392. (Is it merely a clerical error that the entry of Erskine's name in the index of this volume reads: "Erskine, Rev. Thomas, of Linlathen"?)

[4] Geoffrey Rowell has astutely observed that, for Erskine, theology "centered on the point at which Christian doctrines were related to human experience, and consequently...the doctrine

of the future life became closely linked with, if not reduced to [one's] participation in the present." *Hell and the Victorians* (Oxford, 1974), p. 74.

5   On 9 April 1827, Erskine was in Naples and visited the house where his father had died. That evening he wrote to his cousin Rachel: "I have often wished that I had the slightest trace of him in my memory, but I was just two years old when he left home. I know nothing of my father's mind, except very general traits. I don't know how he felt when he knew he was on the borders of the invisible world" (Hanna, p. 92).

6   This was the "Introductory Essay" to the letters of Samuel Rutherford. Since the Essay itself had no connection at all with Rutherford, to it was appended ("by another hand") a few pages designed to make the connection.

7   Olive Brose, *Frederick Denison Maurice: Rebellious Conformist* (Athens, OH: 1971), pp. 42-3.

8   At the end of the century Henry Henderson observed that Erskine's book was "one of the most valuable contributions to the literature of Christian apologetics in the English language." *Erskine of Linlathen: Selections and Biography* (Edinburgh & London, 1899), p. 34.

9   *The Eclectic Review* (New Series), Vol. 16 (July-Dec., 1821), pp. 180-1.

10 Soame Jenyns, *A View of the Internal Evidence of the Christian Religion* (London, 1776), p. 6.

11 John Smyth, "Internal Evidence of Christianity," in *Lectures on the Evidence of Revealed Religion by Ministers of the Established Church in Glasgow* (Glasgow, 1838), p. 361. The tone of Smyth's polemical rhetoric can be seen in his depiction of Thomas Paine's *The Age of Reason*: "The vilest production, perhaps, that ever issued from the bottomless pit of infidelity." *Ibid.*, p. 365.

12 So Henderson, *op. cit.*, p. 31.

13 J.H. Newman, "On the Introduction of Rationalistic Principles into Religion" (*Tracts for the Times*, No. 73) (London, 1836), p. 15.

14 Erskine did comment, however, in a letter dated 10 March 1823, that a friend had told him that "[William] Wilberforce thought the Essay of Faith very obscure...But if he finds it obscure, how many there must be who will find it so too" (Hanna, p. 36).

15 M.D. Conway, *Autobiography: Memories and Experiences* (Boston, 1904), Vol. 2, p. 105.

16 Quoted by W.A. Knight, *op. cit.*, p. 60.

17 Henderson, *op. cit.*, p. ix.

CHAPTER TWO: THE BEGINNINGS OF CONTROVERSY

If Erskine manifested a liking for the writings of John Gambold, the same cannot be said of his attitude towards Richard Baxter's *The Saints' Everlasting Rest*. His friend Thomas Chalmers had persuaded him to write an introductory essay to a new edition of Baxter's classic (to be published by Collins in their "Series of Select Christian Authors"), but Erskine did not find the task an easy one. He even wrote to Chalmers: "I feel afraid of Baxter's Saints' Rest" (Hanna, p. 34). And it is clear why this was so. On the one hand, he attempted to commend Baxter to his readers as a valiant fighter for the truth; on the other hand, there was much in Baxter's book which repelled him. Erskine did in fact write the requested Introduction, but few are the essays in which an author's inner ambivalence is so transparently in evidence. It is as if Erskine were both introducing Baxter to his readers while simultaneously criticizing the very things which Baxter represented. Through this dialectic of commendation and criticism, Erskine's own theological assumptions and predilections were bound to rise to the surface.

Baxter, he wrote, was one of that "glorious army of reformation," made of the "same stern stuff with the Wickliffs, and the Luthers, and the Knoxes, and the Cranmers, and the Latimers of a former age" (Baxter, p. v). These reformers Erskine styled as "enlightened crusaders" who by their labors and sufferings rescued "the key of knowledge from the unworthy hands in which it had long lain rusted and misused" (p. vi). Because they were born in the midst of civil and religious conflict, however, life for them was "warfare," and the "language of strife" was their mother tongue." In this "army" of reformers, Richard Baxter was, Erskine admitted, a "standard-bearer." But, if such militaristic metaphors expressed with some accuracy the contribution which Baxter and others made to the cause of religion, they also pointed to their most obvious short-comings. If life was for them "warfare," they were then consequently given to express in their writings a "severity of rebuke" and a "sternness of denunciation" which, said Erskine, "we are sorry to meet" (p. vi). What he was sorry to meet was, quite specifically, Baxter's lack of compassion. Baxter went into too much detail, for instance, in cataloguing the extreme punishments to be meted out to sinners after their death (a catalogue, it must be said, somewhat in contradistinction to the book's title). It struck Erskine that such threats, however well intended, wrongly suggested that God takes pleasure in affliction. "Let man not use his own words, and far less his own fancy," Erskine wrote, "in describing the future punishments of the impenitent .... There can be no real advantage gained by agitating the imagination on such a subject." And then, quite pointedly, "[M]en are not made Christians by terror but by love" (p. x).

The aggressive tenor of Baxter's work, then, was what disturbed Erskine. Scripture may indeed speak of a "wrath to come," but is it possible to conceive of a God who takes pleasure in the misery of sinners, particularly since such misery, rather than being visited upon them by God, is the result of "the operations of evil principles upon the soul" (p. x)? Erskine thought not. God may threaten, but the "threatenings of God are all expressions of love" (*ibid.*). Had not Baxter totally overlooked, wondered Erskine, those more powerful passages in the Bible which testify to God's enduring and long-suffering compassion? God, in fact, looks yearningly upon his creatures and says: "I cannot bear to lose you ...; come then, and be my friend, and my child" (p. xii).

There is much in what Erskine goes on to say that is theologically unformed and to some extent naïve. And yet, within this short essay are to be found themes and images which will find maturer articulation in Erskine's subsequent writings. Wary of the ever-present danger of antinomianism, for instance, he sketches out, in contradistinction to Baxter's view that pardon and "rest" are the end-state of the Christian pilgrimage, his assertion that pardon has, through Christ's sacrifice, already been pronounced. Erskine was convinced that the biblical doctrine of justification (given precious little attention in Baxter's book) is the "great centre of the Christian system" (p. xv). While human systems "always place pardon, or the divine favor, at the end of the race" (which implies that sin must be removed before the condemnation can be lifted), God's method is first to remove the condemnation so that, in obedient response to such mercy, "men may cease from sinning" (*ibid.*). The real "Saints' Rest," as distinct from Baxter's, rather than being a description exclusively of the future heavenly state, was for Erskine a present reality, although much impeded "by corruption within and sorrow without." "[F]uture glory is not desired by a Christian as an entirely new and hitherto unknown thing, but as the full accomplishment of a blessedness already begun" (p. xxxi). A pardon that has been effected in the past, and a blessedness that is available in the present—these are themes which will be iterated by Erskine with increasing clarity and vigor.

It is clear that, if Baxter's vision of the "Saints' Everlasting Rest" jarred Erskine's sensitivities, at the same time it motivated him to articulate his own perception of that "rest" which is available, not only in the heavenly estate, not only at the time when the final restitution of all things will have been accomplished (when "God is entirely glorified, and entirely loved, and entirely obeyed," and when there will be a "rest from all controversy with God" [Baxter, pp. xxxiii & xxxv]), but available to all those who know *now* that "there is not rest, except in Him who made us" (p. xxxv). This was no new thought to Erskine. Some two years prior to his wrestling with the Baxter essay, Erskine wrote (from Dresden) to his younger sister Christian (Mrs. Charles Stirling) urging her, by way of illustrating the peace enjoyed by those who rest confidently in the gospel, to read one of Archbishop Leighton's sermons. (It is interesting to note that Robert Leighton's family came from Forfarshire, not far from Erskine's estate at Linlathen.) The sermon Erskine recommended was based on the text: "He shall not be afraid of evil tidings; his heart is fixed, trusting in the Lord" (Ps. 112.7). In this sermon Erskine must have discerned an understanding of the gospel that was

CHAPTER TWO: THE BEGINNINGS OF CONTROVERSY

wanting in Leighton's Puritan contemporary, Richard Baxter, and it was a sermon which Erskine said he had "read ... very often and always with great pleasure" (Hanna, p. 32). Undoubtedly he was also very much influenced by it, for, as with Gambold's writings which so emphasized the attribute of Christian joy, in Leighton's Erskine found a celebration of Christian happiness, a happiness which is descriptive of Christian life, and not merely seen as a heavenly reward, after death, for earthly obedience.

"Blessed is the man that feareth the Lord," said the Psalmist (112.1), "that delighteth greatly in his commandments." Just so, thought Leighton; that trusting kind of fear does indeed lead to happiness. But here is another kind of fear, an inappropriate fear born of suspicion or anxiety. It is a fear which, according to Leighton, arises out of doubt, a fear that distrusts God's love. It is an abrasive fear, a constant irritant to the inner eye. How dreary are the lives of those who have to insist of their friends, "Do you love me?" How sad when they are unable to accept the grace-fullness of genuine friendship. And, if so with our friends, how much more so with God. Leighton's point, then, was a simple one, as simple as it was ironic: those who truly fear God shall not be afraid. In the true fear of God, all petty fears are swallowed up; upon those who truly fear God is bestowed a trust and happiness that can look even at death and say, with the Psalmist, "Though I walk through the valley and shadow of death, yet I will fear no evil, for thou art with me" (Psalm 23.4—as quoted by Leighton).[1]

For Erskine, it seems, any doctrine or theological assertion was to be tested against a two-fold criterion: (1) What effect does it have upon us? and (2) What does it say about God? If a doctrine leads us to despair or banishes hope from our consciousness or leads us to believe that there is no escape from condemnation, such a doctrine must be eschewed, and quite specifically because it portrays a God whose vindictive wrath is perceived to outweigh, if not totally obliterate, the divine mercy. On both counts, then, such a doctrine must be rejected. By this criterion, clearly Gambold's emphasis on joy and Leighton's on happiness were to be espoused, while Baxter's want of compassion was to be shunned. Baxter wrote of death as the gateway to possible eternal punishment; Gambold and Leighton knew that death, rather than bringing us to inexorable pain, could be faced with serene confidence because the joy and happiness one has already experienced in this life as having its source in God, can only be experienced to an even larger degree upon the completion of one's earthly pilgrimage.

Eight years after Erskine had commended Leighton's sermon to his sister, her husband Charles died (February 1830). Erskine spoke of his brother-in-law's death as the scene of ... a glorious victory," and to Rachel he wrote:

From the beginning of [Charles'] illness he anticipated the result, and he welcomed it as his Father's summons calling him home. God did great things for him, and during the last days of his life, whilst the struggle was going on, the Good Shepherd never left him for a moment. I was with him the last two days, and heard him say many sweet things, which are now like balm to poor Christian's heart" (Hanna, pp. 124ff).

And to James Stirling, Erskine wrote the same day, telling him that Charles had said, shortly before he died, that his soul was "full of peace and joy in the Lord, that God is all light, and no darkness at all." Charles then turned to Erskine and said, "It has just come to me like a flash that you were right about these things" (Hanna, p. 126).

"These things" undoubtedly refers to Erskine's perception and experience of the infinite extent of God's compassion, a perception that he had been articulating with increasing clarity and intensity between 1822 (when he commended Leighton's sermon to Christian) and 1830 (when Christian's husband died). It was a period during which his letters of consolation and his theological assertions became two different ways of speaking of the same conviction, i.e., the "universality" of Christ's atonement. As he wrote to Rachel:

You have told me that you believe that "Christ is the propitiation for the sins of the whole world," in the obvious sense of these words. You have told me that it is God's message to this world of prodigals, that this is the message which is the power of God unto salvation to all who believe it. Well, do you know that this doctrine is looked upon as a heresy by almost all the teachers of religion in this country, and that a directly opposite doctrine is preached? If you believe in the universality of the atonement, you must believe that the limitation of it is a falsification of the record which God has given us concerning his Son ... God's message to the world is not delivered whilst a limited atonement is preached; and as long as this erroneous interpretation is preached from our orthodox pulpits, the people may have the Bible in their hands, but the unfaithful interpretation will be a veil on their hearts in the reading of it. (Hanna, p. 107f.)

Charles Stirling may have believed Erskine to have been "right about these things," and Rachel Erskine may have shared her cousin Thomas' views, but this letter surely suggests that the "severity of rebuke" and "sternness of denunciation" of which Erskine had complained in Baxter's writings was soon to be directed against himself. It was the publication in 1828 of his *The Unconditional Freeness*

CHAPTER TWO: THE BEGINNINGS OF CONTROVERSY 17

of the Gospel which drew the initial, if somewhat guarded criticism, while the subsequent publication in 1830 of his Introductory Essay to *Extracts of Letters to a Christian Friend by a Lady* elicited from a host of critics a response that was increasingly hostile and vituperative. There were indeed some who praised the former work. F.D. Maurice, for instance, spoke of how positively influential it had been on his own thinking,[2] and Erskine's friend Thomas Chalmers, "in his greathearted way, gave it [a] cordial welcome."[3] This welcome, however, was not without its irony for two reasons. First of all, Chalmers characterized the work as "the *Marrow of Modern Divinity* modernised."[4] But the anonymously written book of that title, published first in 1645 and then again in 1719, had been condemned by the General Assembly of the Church of Scotland in 1720 because it contained views antithetical to strict Calvinism: assurance was of the essence of faith, the atonement is universally effective for all persons, holiness is not necessary to salvation, and the fear of punishment and the hope of reward are not proper motives for obedience. If, then, these ancient views were heretical, was not Erskine, one might ask, also a heretic? Perhaps even Chalmers, for all his respect for Erskine, thought so, for he is reported to have remarked "that the train of his thoughts might ultimately lead Erskine to doubt the eternity of future punishment. Now that would be going sadly against Scripture."[5] Whether or not Erskine's views were "against Scripture," Chalmers was certainly accurate in his prediction! The faithful Alexandre Vinet, however, was able, in reflecting on Erskine's involvement in controversy, to write in admiration of his *ami écossais* and at the same time to embrace his alleged "heretical views":

> Il est grandement hérétique, dit-on, mais c'est un bien bon chrétien.
> Il n'avait rien qui appelât la discussion; sa conversation était sérieuse sans raideur, nourrie des faits et d'aperçus, et il était rare qu'on le quittâ sans être riche de quelque idée nouvelle.[6]

Yet it was precisely Erskine's *idées nouvelles* which most disturbed his critics, convinced as they were that "novelty" and "heresy" are synonymous terms (as even Erskine himself had suggested at the end of his *Internal Evidence*!). As one critic put it: "I don't like the new wine, for I feel that the old is better."[7]

Erskine himself cannot have been unaware that his newly published *Unconditional Freeness* would draw forth negative comments (in spite of Hanna's observation [p. 100] that "its author was not prepared for so cordial a reception of this volume by some, still less for so severe a reprobation of it by others."). It is clear from a reading of the 1828 and 1830 publications that Erskine was quite consciously and intentionally controverting both the received doctrines of the Church of Scotland as well as much of the theological posture of that body. Its doctrine was unswervingly Calvinistic and its posture as narrow as it was unbending. As early as 1826 he had observed that "religion in Scotland is too much a thing of science, and too little a thing of personal application and interest" (Hanna, p. 56), while the following year he wrote to Chalmers: "May the Lord ... send an awakening spirit to arouse and vivify the torpid Church of Scotland" (Hanna, p. 98). By the time of the publication of his *Unconditional Freeness* and the "Introductory Essay" to *Extracts*, Erskine was openly making statements which were sure to garner rebuke. But even when that rebuke came, he could say "... in spite of [some people's] strong dissent, I feel more and more convinced that I have followed the word of God in describing the Gospel" (Hanna, p. 109). The question which Erskine raised was whether pardon was dependent on a person's faith or whether faith was the appropriation of a pardon already bestowed. Because he felt that "[F]orgiveness is a permanent condition of the heart of God" (Freeness, p. 57), he opted, as he had previously in his Introduction to Baxter, for the latter. If the former, then faith is a "work," and forgiveness a "reward." Or, as he put it, "[T]he promise of pardon, as a reward of faith, seems to me a mere human invention, in direct opposition to the whole tenor of the Gospel" (Freeness, p. 73). Erskine's conviction that pardon was a past action on the part of God, to which we are invited to respond, meant that it would be blasphemous to suggest that God offers pardon to some and not to others. The good news of forgiveness, because it is rooted in God's unchanging love, must be good news for all people. This is what Erskine meant by the "unconditional gratuitousness" of the gospel and by the "universality" both of the gospel declaration (*to* all people) and of God's eternal purpose (*for* all people). God's love is not an elective love but a disinterested love, "waiting there with a patience grieved but not exhausted by the madly pertinacious rejection which meets it" (Freeness, p. 140). Such a view leads necessarily, as it did for Erskine, to an assertion as to the final "restitution of all things," an assertion, he said, which "occupies a much less space in the usual preaching of the gospel and in the thoughts of men, than it ought to do" (Freeness, p. 51).

In Andrew Thomson's preaching, however, such a gospel held no space at all. In 1811 he had founded the *Edinburgh Christian Instructor* in order to alert the unwary to theological aberrations wherever they might be found and, as minister of St. George's Church in Edinburgh, his pulpit became the self-styled beacon of Westminster orthodoxy. Thomson was soon to become Erskine's most hostile critic, but his review of *Unconditional Freeness* was irenic in tone. Claiming respect for Erskine's "deep piety and devoted attention to the cause of pure and undefiled Christianity," he did point to some "errors" which may injure or perplex the unsuspecting. He pointed, for instance (not surprisingly), to Erskine's "fanciful, unwarrantable, and dangerous innovations." These "innovations" had to do with the "new meanings" which Erskine gave to such concepts as justification, heaven and hell, salvation, and eternal life. Having listed his objections to the volume, Thomson ended his review on a conciliatory note:

> [T]hough we differ widely from Mr. Erskine in many of his positions, we like exceedingly the manner in which he has

conducted his Treatise. There are an ease and an elegance and a felicity in the diction, and a glowing spirit of Christian piety and benevolence in the sentiments, which cannot but make the happiest impression on the mind of every Christian reader.[8]

Not all reviewers were as restrained in their criticism. An anonymous Church of England cleric, for instance, published this pointed parody of *Unconditional Freeness*:

> According to [Erskine], justification does not consist in receiving pardon of God, on believing and embracing the Gospel, but in attaining to a sense of pardon *already* granted. The pardon has long ago been proclaimed, and it is perfectly universal. There lives not a human being, whether Saint, or Savage, or Sage, to whom the plenary and gratuitous forgiveness is not at this moment extended. The amnesty is so comprehensive, that none are [*sic*] excluded; so free and gratuitous, that neither faith or obedience are required, as conditions, of those who would take advantage of it. The whole world, therefore, is at this moment, actually, and freely forgiven; but a very small part of the world know, or believe, or care anything about the matter.[9]

Thomson it was, though, who was to become the heresy hunter *par excellence*. How ironic, then, that it is precisely in the volume concerning which his remarks were relatively mild that Erskine's own definition of Heresy is to be found: "It is not by philosophy or speculation that we can know God, but by the desire of the heart after Him ... There is no true religion except the holy love of God abiding in the heart; and there is no heresy so great as the want of love" (*Freeness*, p. 132). God's forgiving love is indeed universal, but why, wondered Erskine, do not more people receive it into their hearts? Because of human pride. The very gratuitousness of the gospel offends our pride; it offends that element in us which with "perverse ingenuity" would oppose self to God and claim independence from God. Self is the great anti-Christ. What one can find only in God's forgiving love, the selfish person looks for within the compass of human capabilities, but in vain. How ironic that Erskine's view of universality drew charges of antinomianism, whereas his experience of Scottish preaching led him to see pride at its root and a more pernicious antinomianism as its fruit. If pardon has already been bestowed, quipped Erskine's detractors, will not sin the more abound? Or, as one of them put it: "Did you ever hear Mr. Erskine pray for the forgiveness of sins, or of his transgressions, or of his iniquities? You certainly have; and we would ask again, Is not this betraying his unbelief of the sentiments he publicly professes and avows?"[10] This question was to be raised in a variety of ways by several critics, but behind it was the almost frenetic fear that, if the universality of forgiveness were to be proclaimed and, even more, to be believed, then all the theological and institutional structures of Christianity would come toppling down. John Smyth, for instance, was passionate in this respect. He openly attacked Erskine's "numerous delusions ... none of which exceeds in absurdity the new, or rather modernised doctrine of universal forgiveness."[11] It is a doctrine, he went on to say, which "dishonours the electing grace" of the Father, the "redeeming grace of the Son," and the "renovating grace of the Holy Spirit." More than this, it "opposes the moral supremacy" of God, "removes many powerful motives to a life of faith and holiness," and "rests on principles of biblical interpretation which are alike untenable and dangerous." "Bright visions" of salvation for all may be "delightful to anticipate," but "our hopes must not exceed, or interfere with, the recorded declarations of the inspired Word."[12]

William Hamilton, Minister of Strathblane, was no less explicit (in a work dedicated to Andrew Thomson!):

> We boldly and openly tell our hearers, that, till they believe on Christ for their own salvation, instead of being redeemed and pardoned, they are the children of disobedience and wrath, in the gall of bitterness and bond of iniquity. We leave this awful truth to work in their guilty consciences, till, by the blessing of the Holy Ghost, they are roused from their dreadful lethargy, and compelled to flee the wrath to come ... But to tell one and all, that Christ has redeemed them; that their sins are forgiven ... this is to administer the strongest opiate that delusion can supply to lull secure and carnal consciences to rest.[13]

"If Mr. Erskine had earned our confidence as a theological writer," wrote yet another critic, "it does not follow that he should retain that confidence when we contemplate him as the victim of specious and delusive errors."[14]

That Erskine was said to be the "victim" of such errors may be an intentional suggestion that he had been duped or at least unduly influenced by John McLeod Campbell (see Ch. 3), but, in any event, the growing body of criticism against Erskine was to pillory him no longer as the "victim" of such specious errors but as the "author" of them.

It was James Buchanan, minister of the parish in North Lieth, who responded to Erskine's *Unconditional Freeness* with the most fervent and sustained animadversions, arguing his case with constant reference to scriptural texts. "Not one passage can be adduced from Scripture," he wrote, "to prove that Christ dies for **all men**. If any passage there be, let it be produced. Assuredly, it is not to be found in your book."[15] He complained, as had Thomson, that Erskine used old terms in new ways, albeit in a book whose style was exquisite. "It is a holy book ... But the fascinations of its eloquence may render even its errors popular, and

CHAPTER TWO: THE BEGINNINGS OF CONTROVERSY

never is religion in greater danger than when any of its distinguished advocates deviate from the simple truth of the Bible."[16]

As I have already indicated, it was Erskine's Introductory Essay to *Extracts*,[17] more than his *Unconditional Freeness*, upon which a storm of abuse was laid. In this essay, Erskine distilled and brought into sharper focus much of what he had said in the 1828 publication. There are two major differences, however. First of all, while the assertion of universal pardon is maintained, greater emphasis than before is placed on what is commonly referred to as the "doctrine of personal assurance." Secondly, in a way he had not previously done, Erskine is quite specific in naming the opponents against whom he is arguing. There is, he wrote, the religion of God; but opposed to it is the "religion of the land." This latter is a religion born of selfishness, a religion which seeks not who God is but what one may get from God. It is a religion which urges us to seek heaven so as to avoid hell. It is a religion concerned to strike a mercenary "bargain with God," with no provision for "love towards God." It is a religion which perceives God as either the powerful bestower of benefits or the inflicter of injury. It is a religion which misconstrues faith, leads to self-righteousness, and refuses to tell us that our sins have been forgiven. Too, it is a religion whose adherents abhor the doctrine of assurance because (1) they realize that they do not have the fruits of the Spirit, because (2) they believe (erroneously) that such fruits are the necessary warrants of assurance, and because (3) they believe that, since assurance is necessary to salvation, they cannot be saved. The "religion of the land," in fact, makes God a liar. "This," concluded Erskine, "I believe to be the prevalent religion of the land,—taught from the pulpits and received by the people ... This may be a harsh and presumptuous saying, but I feel it to be the kindest thing that I can say, because I am persuaded that it is the truth" (Lady, p. xxi). And then, with even more ardor (whether "harsh" or "kind"), he equates the "false gospel" of human invention with a

> leprosy which has overspread the land. And whence does it proceed? It proceeds from the voice of the shepherds who tell the people that, although the gospel is a proclamation of God's love, and of forgiveness of sins through Christ—yet that those only who are loved, and those only who are forgiven, who have faith in the gospel. (Lady, p. xxiii)

The "shepherds," of course, took offence at this, and soon pamphlets and reviews and even books were written to defend the "religion of the land." (A large number of these responses were written anonymously, many of them using such exotic noms-de-plume as "Anglicanus," "Juvenal," "Anti-Gallicus," "Verus," etc.) They saw in Erskine, not only a "lay" theologian whose doctrinal assertions were suspect, but a person who had too proudly and too presumptuously challenged the integrity of the whole ecclesial establishment. The furor that ensued can hardly have been avoided, and many were the stalwart who came to the church's defense. Not surprisingly, Andrew Thomson was the most prominent of these. Thomson thrived on controversy. Of him one historian (in a sentence of severe complexity) wrote:

> He will not be forgotten; nor will he soon cease to be spoken of in those terms which the world, whether religious or secular, lavishes on the man who for a time occupied a place as a controversialist so eminent, that his success in stripping bare an antagonist—and often with little of the milk of human kindness in the act—was rewarded by having his own nakedness in some of those things, that mark the milder spirit of the minister of peace and charity, overlooked and palliated, if not with some of his enthusiastic admirers, even applauded as a virtue.[18]

And a colleague of Thomson's, a certain Dr. Thomas McCrie, said, "When convinced of the justice of a cause ... [Thomson] threw his whole soul into it, summoned all his powers to its defence, and assailed its adversaries, not only with strong argument, but with sharp, pointed, and poignant sarcasm."[19]

Thomson's response to Erskine was indeed sharp, pointed, and sarcastic, and with little of the milk of human kindness. It was published as *The Doctrine of Universal Pardon*, and consisted of twelve sermons (covering 363 pages) and a series of thirty-three appendices (covering an additional 129 pages). His personal animosity towards Erskine now found full voice. He claimed the purpose of his own volume to be to "guard the young, the unwary, the unexperienced, who are still sound in the faith, against the danger of infection, and to provide them with adequate means of safety." And he was unambiguous as to the nature of the "infection": Erskine's was a "deadly heresy," his views "egregiously wrong." He was guilty of "gross and palpable inconsistency," while his writings led to the "most absurd and pernicious consequences." There were in his books such "inaccuracy of thinking, such feebleness of argument, such a destitution of all those high qualities ... which authorise a man to come forward as a reformer of Biblical Theology," that one can only see in his assertions an "indiscriminating and reckless vehemence," an "arrogance and violence," as well as "perverse interpretations of Scripture, unsubstantiated averments, false representations, and confused, misty, unintelligible paragraphs, for which there is no name in our books of rhetoric." His attempt to lay the "whole Christian world" (e.g., Scotland!) under his ban contains "such uncharitableness, such wrathful declamation, such narrow-minded bigotry, such assumptions of exclusive knowledge ..." that everything he says is "destructive to the interests of morality" and "ensnaring and ruinous to immortal souls." Yet, perhaps aware that his own rhetoric had been somewhat too effusive, Thomson concluded, in a statement perhaps too ingenuous, "The ministers and people of this country are really very much indebted to Mr. Erskine for his

CHAPTER TWO: THE BEGINNINGS OF CONTROVERSY

warnings, rebukes, and exhortations, severe though they may be, and ending though they do in a curse. I have no disposition to curse him in return."[20]

Andrew Thomson, of course, was not Erskine's sole detractor. Archibald Robertson joined the ranks of his critics and wrote a large book (a "Helpful book but too big for the ordinary reader," wrote one reviewer[21]) entitled *A Vindication of the "Religion of the Land,"* in which he attacked the whole of Erskine's "system" from the first of his publications through his pamphlet on "The Gifts of the Spirit" (1830; see Ch. 4). In his *Essay on Faith* and *Internal Evidence*, said Robertson, Erskine's errors were then in progress, but such errors were hidden under the cover of the author's practical piety. Yet, with the publication of *Unconditional Freeness* and the Introduction to *Extracts*, the veil is drawn back and Erskine's theological heterodoxy is seen for what it is. At the end of *Unconditional Freeness*, Erskine had disavowed any wish to excite controversy, but, said Robertson, "you have done just that!"

> You condemn the religion and the religious professors of the land ... [yet] you dread a pitched battle. Like a scouting party you are ever in motion, and brandish the weapons of defiance at a distance, and if by accident you are brought into close combat, feeling the strength of the enemy, you retreat to your camp, and fight from your entrenchments.[22]

In reviewing the whole of Erskine's "system," Robertson's primary target was what he perceived to be Erskine's radical departure from the received "doctrine of election." Not only had Erskine denied eternal election (along with the Arminians), he had gone even beyond the Arminians in portraying a God whose law is a relaxed law and whose righteous demands are erroneously conceived to destroy the freedom of moral agency and are thus to be equated with "iron-handed Necessity or the Blind Destiny of the Stoics." To this Robertson opposed, in a careful encapsulation of Chapter III of the *Westminster Confession*, what he felt to be the true "scriptural" view:

> God did from eternity, by the most wise and holy counsel of his own will, and for the manifestation of his glory, freely and unalterably predestinate a certain number of our race to everlasting life. The rest of mankind, God, in the exercise of the same sovereign pleasure which induced him to fore-ordain a certain number to eternal happiness, was pleased not to elect but to pass by; and all whom he has so passed by will receive the punishment of their sins in a future state ... This decree of God, however, neither affects the free agency of man, so as to destroy his accountability, nor makes God in any sense the author of sin.[23]

If Mr. Erskine is unable to understand such a doctrine, Robertson added, it is not on that account false! The anonymous reviewer of Robertson's book claimed that the author had "demolished the theories of the antagonist in a very masterly style" and praised him for having turned "our attention to all the leading errors that have been propounded by that unfortunate intruder into the regions of theology—Mr. Thomas Erskine, whose name has sunk into a mere index for whatever is rash, silly, extravagant, and unscriptural in doctrinal statement."[24]

There is no need to add to this dreary catalogue of angry responses to Erskine's as not yet fully developed theological challenges to traditional Scottish orthodoxy. The doctrinal issues at stake were clear. The thrust of his assertion as to universal pardon or personal assurance lay not so much in its "novelty" (many had said as much before) but in its manifest opposition to the Calvinistic doctrine of a limited atonement. Nor was Erskine guilty of the charge of holding "unscriptural views"; both sides, as always, could cite texts in support of their positions and interpret the Bible as their prejudices directed.[25] It may in fact be the case that doctrinal or scriptural arguments, for all their vehemence, concealed some deeper hidden causes for the conflict between Erskine and his critics. Erskine was indeed dissatisfied with the "religion of the land," but his dissatisfaction arose, it would seem, not so much out of specific points of doctrine as out of his increasing conviction that formal religion in Scotland was a static thing, unmoved and unmoving. The living and compassionate God who lay at the heart of Erskine's religious sensitivities was not a God who, when distant, was beyond human reach or discernment, or, when close, was terrifying. At the center of the controversy, then, were two distinct theological postures, neither of them defined, illuminated, nor exhausted by recourse to doctrinal or scriptural authority. Which leads one to conclude that, on the surface, Erskine and his opponents understood each other very well, but, beneath the surface, there was a chronic inability to understand or appreciate what the other was trying to say. That the charges laid against Erskine were excessively vehement goes without saying, as does the acrimony with which Erskine directed his blanket condemnations against the established church and its "shepherds." It cannot be said that Erskine was more charitable than his critics. The "gentle" Erskine was not always that gentle.[26]

May not the question of ecclesial "status" also have been one of the hidden causes behind the controversy, a cause seldom alluded to and even less often mentioned? Erskine was a layman, a lawyer by training, and therefore without any recognized theological credentials. He was an "intruder into the regions of theology," whereas the ministers of the Kirk had sustained rigorous and disciplined study in scripture, theology, and related subjects. They could have hardly taken an untrained layman's criticisms with equanimity. Nor could they enter into genuine theological discussion with him with any degree of mutuality, for they were not equals. Professional honor was at stake. One cleric there was who even pleaded with Erskine to be "more sparing of his *reckless accusations of many whom God had raised and honoured to be the instruments of bringing many sons and daughters to glory.*"[27]

If, reflected in such a statement, there was at issue the question of clerical vs. lay "status," closely related to it was the matter of clerical **control**. The "shepherds" were self-consciously aware of their responsibility to exercise authoritative oversight in respect to the morals of the men and women ("sheep") in their congregations. Erskine, they believe, tended to dispute that authority and to preach a kind of liberalism that would inevitably lead to license. If control were wrested from the hands of those duly appointed to be the guardians of the faith and the arbiters of individual and corporate morality, an epidemic of profligacy was sure to ensue.[28] A contemporary sermon by David Davidson, Minister of the Chapel of Ease in Broughty Ferry, makes this eminently clear:

> But let [the doctrine of universal pardon] once be received by the sceptical and the licentious, the ignorant and the ungodly, and such must, of necessity, be the miserable result. Let them only be taught and persuaded that their past transgressions are all forgiven, that the iniquities which they are now committing are all forgiven, that the greatest and the most abominable crimes which they have the power to perpetrate are all forgiven; and then, what is to be expected, but that their consciences should become altogether remorseless, and their passions should break forth without any control save the laws of the civil society, and their lives should be disgraced and their souls destroyed by every species of iniquity and every gradation of guilt?[29]

If there were overtly doctrinal reasons for the controversy between Erskine and his critics, as well as those more elusive causes for the acrimonious nature of it, the controversy was nevertheless a tragic one. If his accusers were deeply offended by what Erskine had written, Erskine himself must have been deeply hurt by what they said of him (although he never responded in writing to their attacks). And one cannot but wonder how he felt when, upon the publication of his *Unconditional Freeness*, it turned out to be a book which "so ill accorded with the religious tenets of Dr. Russell" [*sic*],[30] the Minister of Ward Chapel (Congregational), of which Erskine was then a member, that he asked Erskine to withdraw from the communion of his church.[31] And, indeed, Erskine did withdraw, "and worshipped afterwards with the Episcopalians."[32] But he did not withdraw from the heat of controversy. His friendship with and support of John McLeod Campbell, the author of the so-called "Row heresy," was soon to involve him in a guilt-by-association relationship. Further, his publication of a slim pamphlet entitled *The Gifts of the Spirit*, written in support of the so-called "West Country Miracles," was to elicit even harsher response than had his previous publications. The

Edinburgh Christian Instructor was to have ample material for its forthcoming issues, much of it generating considerably more heat than light.

Notes to Chapter Two

1. *The Works of Robert Leighton* (Edinburgh, 1843), pp. 407-8.
2. See, for instance, the Dedication (to Erskine) in his *The Prophets and Kings of the Old Testament* (London, 1894), pp. v-xii.
3. Henderson, *op. cit.*, p. 35.
4. *Ibid.*
5. Quoted without reference by William Hanna, *Memoirs of the Life and Writings of Thomas Chalmers* [by his son-in-law], (New York: Harper & Brothers, 1850-1852), Vol. III, p. 252. John Roxborough, however, has said that Chalmers was in fact sympathetic to the reasons which had led his friend Erskine in the direction of "universalism," and that Chalmers himself had been "accused of holding the same opinions." "Chalmer's Theology of Mission," in A.C. Cheyne (ed.), *The Practical and the Pious: Essays on Thomas Chalmers (1790-1847)* (Edinburgh: The Saint Andrew Press, 1985), p. 177.
6. Quoted by E. Rambert, *Alexandre Vinet: Histoire de sa vie et de ses ouvrages* (Lausanne, 1876, 3rd ed.), t. 2, p. 45.
7. Anon., *An Examination and Refutation* (Edinburgh, 1830), p. 44.
8. [Andrew Thomson], "Review of the Unconditional Freeness of the Gospel...by Thomas Erskine," *Edinburgh Christian Instructor*, Vol. 27, No. 6 (June, 1828), pp. 410-27.
9. *The British Critic* (Vol. 5, 1829), pp. 61-2.
10. Anon. [James Russel?], *A Letter to a Friend, on Universal Pardon, as advanced by Thomas Erskine, Esq., and Others* (Dundee, 1830), p. 11.
11. John Smyth, *A Treatise on the Forgiveness of Sins as the Privilege of the Redeemed; in Opposition to the Doctrine of Universal Pardon* (Glasgow, 1830), p. 2.
12. *Ibid., passim.*
13. William Hamilton, *Remarks on Certain Opinions Propagated, Respecting Universal Redemption* (Glasgow, 1830), pp. 29-30.
14. *A Letter to a Friend, op. cit.*, p. 12. It is difficult, in the lights of these and similar criticisms--most of them from Ministers of the Church of Scotland--to discern what Henderson (*op. cit.*, p. 35) meant when he wrote that *Freeness* "attained a high place among the better class [sic] of religious people."
15. [James Buchanan], *A Letter to Thomas Erskine, Esq.* (Edinburgh, 1828), p. 10. In the British Library copy of this work an unknown reader has written in the margin opposite this passage, "Indeed!" and followed it with a string of biblical references.
16. *Ibid.*, pp. 22-3.
17. This essay was republished in 1874, long after the original controversy had died down, as *True and False Religion*, in the Preface to which (p. iii) the anonymous editor referred to another, obviously less edifying, controversy: This little book "cannot fail to be of service to

CHAPTER TWO: THE BEGINNINGS OF CONTROVERSY   27

many...especially when the Church of England is distracted by debate about rubrics relating to vestments and postures"[!].

[18] James Bryce, *Ten Years of the Church of Scotland from 1833 to 1843* (Edinburgh & London, 1850), Vol. 1, p. 243. The inveterate biographer, Jean Watson, tells of the Minister--a keen fisherman--who said to Thomson, "I wonder you spend so much time on your sermons, with your ability and ready speech. Many's the time when I've written a sermon and killed a salmon before breakfast." "Well, sir," replied Thomson, "I'd rather have eaten your salmon than listened to your sermon!" *Life of Andrew Thomson* (Edinburgh, 1882), p. 24. Thomson's reputation as a powerful preacher was wide enough even to find its way into the folk poetry of the Ettrick Shepherd (James Hogg); see his "The First Sermon," in David Groves (ed.), *James Hogg: Tales of Love and Mystery* (Edinburgh: Canongate, 1985), pp. 159-62.

[19] Watson *op. cit.*, pp. 95-6. Henderson has observed, wryly, that "Scotsmen have never relished their spiritual food too highly seasoned. They have a strong distaste for the element of enthusiasm and religious assurance. They have enjoyed a religion that they could argue and fight over." *The Religious Controversies of Scotland* (Edinburgh, 1905), p. 148.

[20] A. Thomson, *The Doctrine of Universal Pardon Considered and Refuted* (Edinburgh, 1830), p. 446 and *passim*. The "curse" to which he refers may be this sentence toward the end of Erskine's essay (p. lxxii): "Who is he that will say to his Maker, thou hast not done all that thou mightest have done? Who is he that will say that, it is because *God will not*, therefore *man does not*? Who is he? Alas! potsher of the earth. Jesus weeps for him."

[21] Anon. [Thomson?], *"Review of A Vindication of the Religion of the Land,"* Edinburgh Christian Instructor, Vol. 29, No. 7 (July, 1830), p. 502.

[22] A. Robertson, *A Vindication of "The Religion of the Land" from Misrepresentations* (Edinburgh, 1830), pp. 5, 9.

[23] *Ibid.*, p. 178 and *passim.*

[24] "Review of A Vindication of the Land," pp. 502-3.

[25] One of Erskine's (and Campbell's) supporters responded to Robert Burns' accusation that Erskine perverted scriptures by saying, that everyone, on no matter what side of the argument, has the capacity to pervert scripture! [Thomas Carlyle], *Protestant Truths and Popish Errors* (Greenock, 1830), p. 9.

[26] Henderson (*Erskine of Linlathen*, pp. 43-4) appears to have overlooked the argumentative and sometimes petulant nature of Erskine's writing: "Many of the matters on which Erskine wrote had been for long in Scotland subjects of heated controversy, and had been written about in angry unchristian manner--in the *"thou vain heretic and runagate"* temper...Erskine introduced a new spirit into the controversial arena, and wrote of his own and his opponents' liability to err."

[27] *An Examination and Refutation*, p. 39 (italics in the original).

[28] This is certainly implied by Thomson (*The Doctrine of Universal Pardon*, p. 238): "The doctrine [which Erskine teaches] is that of universal pardon,--meaning that unbelievers, impenitent persons, hardened profligates, have all their sins, including those they may hereafter commit, already and actually forgiven."

[29] David Davidson, *A Sermon on Acts x.43* (Dundee, 1830), p. 24.

30 Russel responded to Erskine's book with his own *The Way of Salvation, A Discourse by the Rev. Mr. Russel of Dundee; with Notes and Illustrations, containing Remarks on the Doctrine of Universal Pardon* (Dundee, 1830).

31 J. Malcolm, *The Parish in Monifieth in Ancient and Modern Times* (Edinburgh & London, 1910), p. 376.

32 *Ibid.*

CHAPTER THREE: THE ROW HERESY

Although they had most likely met earlier,[1] the first recorded meeting between Erskine and John McLeod Campbell was in the winter of 1828. The occasion was a service in Edinburgh at which Campbell, since September of 1825 the Minister of the parish of Row (Rhu), delivered the sermon. Erskine was in the congregation and his response to the sermon was immediate: "I have heard today from that pulpit," he remarked to a companion, "what I believe to be the true gospel" (Hanna, p. 102). Campbell and Erskine were to see more of each other, and very soon they would become close friends. Erskine, in fact, spent portions of the next two summers in a cottage in Row, a town situated on the eastern shore of the Gareloch[2] in Dumbartonshire. There is no remaining evidence as to what Campbell said in his Edinburgh sermon, but it is fair to assume that what Erskine experienced as the "true Gospel" had something to do with the universality of forgiveness and with "assurance" as being of the essence of faith, for these two men had both arrived independently at a common understanding of these theological positions,[3] so much so that it is impossible to discern who influenced whom; it would appear that the influence was mutual, as was their growing respect and admiration for each other.[4]

So closely were these two friends identified with each other, and so similar were their theological convictions, that it is no surprise that the attacks which had been directed against Erskine would soon find in Campbell a convenient target against which the "orthodox" could rail. There was a difference, however. Whereas Erskine was beyond the reach of ecclesiastical action, by virtue of his being a layman, Campbell, an ordained Minister of the Kirk, could (and did) become the object of official censure. Too, Erskine was not only a layman, he was also a "dissenter." For this reason one of Campbell's critics was constrained to write to him:

> "... we have *our* flocks to watch over, and when modern theorists come among us, and tell our people that we are not preaching the gospel to them, it is high time that we should inquire as to the charge, and the authors and abettors of it. Mr. Erskine is a dissenter, and is therefore at full liberty to say and print what he pleases; You, Sir, are a clergyman of the Church of Scotland, and bound by *solemn vows* not to 'endeavor, directly or indirectly, the subversion of the doctrine, discipline, and government of the church' which feeds and clothes you."[5]

So it was in respect to a Minister of the establishment that the machinery of the ecclesiastical courts directed its attention. The express goal was to root out what was soon to be called the "Row heresy," and, if possible, to depose its author. William Hanna, who was later to become more sympathetic to the views of Campbell and Erskine, described the former as a "young minister of ardent piety, but of slender theological discrimination, [who], in preaching on the extent of the atonement, in asserting that all men's sins were pardoned, and in insisting on assurance of personal salvation as being of the very essence of saving faith, was teaching doctrines at variance with the standards of the Church."[6] By his lack of "theological discrimination," Hanna presumably meant that Campbell was, perhaps naïvely, unaware that his preaching was bound, given the theological tenor of the day, to raise doubts as to his orthodoxy. Yet, as one historian has noted, with characteristic enthusiasm, "[For] the finer orthodoxy of the heart, for sweetness and charm of disposition, no Church in Scotland has produced his equal."[7] Yet at the time not all of Campbell's contemporaries were so charitably disposed. There is the delightful vignette, for instance, about (of all people!) Erskine's gardener who is reported to have said, "And then there was Mr. Campbell of Row; he was a very gude [sic] man, but then he devairged." To which Erskine responded, "As if, after that, there was no more to be said for him!"[8] More sustained and serious criticisms took the form of hastily written articles, reviews, and pamphlets, the majority of them excoriating Campbell and his views, and employing a rhetoric of controversy not dissimilar to that directed against Erskine. And in all of this barrage, Erskine and Campbell are indiscriminately linked. Robert Burns, for instance, asked Campbell:

> What have you gained by your theory [of universal pardon]? Mr. Erskine tells us he has got by it a noble answer to the far-famed argument that evangelical preachers *build up* by one hand what they *pull down* by another; that while they set aside works as the foundation of hope, they introduce in their stead *Christ* and *faith in him*; and thus, in effect, substitute one modification for another; and *universal pardon* puts a negative on all this. Miserable sophistry! Wretched quibbling![9]

Burns also exchanged lengthy (published) letters with Thomas Carlyle, the Edinburgh advocate who defended Campbell at his trial (and who wrote modestly as "A Lay Member of the Church of Scotland"). In the course of the correspondence, Burns decried the "disciples of the Gairloch [sic] neology" for their "modern discoveries" and then went on to say:

> This afternoon in conversing with an intelligent lay-friend, he put to me the question—"What does Mr. Erskine intend by the 'unconditional *freeness* of the gospel,' when his whole system implies, that unless *upon condition* of taking *his view* of the matter, we cannot be saved at all?" I could not tell him. Perhaps you may.[10]

The anonymous (English) reviewer of various writings on the Row Heresy also associated Erskine "and his less gifted coadjutors" with Campbell's views. The Row heretics, he said, were examples of "so much talent combined with so little judgment, so much strength of mind and character united with so much calm puerility or childish vehemence ... Mr. Erskine is unhappily a case in point." Arguing against the thesis of *Unconditional Freeness*, he asserted:

> Forgiveness cannot precede the actual offence; and therefore, although the scheme and purpose of the Divine Mercy, originating in the glorious Perfection of the Divine character, date from before the foundation of the world, yet to represent the actual forgiveness of the human race, and consequently to every individual, as being a past act, antecedent to either the existence of sin of the parties forgiven—is something worse than an anachronism; it is a palpable solecism.[11]

In the midst of this attack and counter-attack, and throughout the trial that was to ensue, Erskine stayed by his "co-religionist," offering him counsel and support, but he wrote nothing bearing directly on the Row heresy. Others, however, came to Campbell's defense. As already noted, the "Lay Member" wrote lengthy epistles to Robert Burns arguing that Campbell's views were not "novel" but could be found in all the great Reformers. There were other sympathetic writers as well. J. Leslie, for instance, wrote a clever pamphlet with the interesting title, *The "Christian Instructor" Instructed*, in which he took issue specifically with the redoubtable Andrew Thomson and his journal. In claiming that the "Bible nowhere teaches that Christ restores all mankind," said Leslie, Thomson had become guilty of a "still more dangerous heresy" than the one with which he had charged Campbell.[12] And while Leslie argued against Thomson, as well as against the unnecessarily polemical tone of the *Edinburgh Christian Instructor*, the anonymous author of a tract called *Candour; or an Impartial Examination of the Row Heresy* addressed the issues of the controversy itself. The accusers of Mr. Campbell, wrote the author,

> allege that he teaches the doctrine of Universal Pardon or Atonement; and that from such a doctrine, or from his mode of enforcing it, it would follow that the Moral Law was divested of its penalties—in other words, that his doctrine is Antinomian. Again, they accuse him of teaching that Assurance belongs to the essence of Faith ... And it is inferred from such a doctrine, that while some enthusiasts may delude themselves with a fancy of being safe, sincere Christians might be driven to despair by it.[13]

The author then proceeds to point out that, although Campbell's critics were correct in respect to what it was that Campbell taught, the implications they drew from those alleged doctrines were not correct. There is no need, he said, to make the "grace of God" an "excuse for licentiousness."[14] Yet the author of *Candour* was less concerned with the specificities of the doctrines under examination than with the rigidity of argument manifested in the writings of Campbell's opponents. This is due, he said, to their "love of system"; too often they are given to "expatiate upon some favourite and systematic view," and are therefore unable to tolerate others who might express themselves differently. It is the "technical forms of dogmatic theology" which get the "Doctors of Divinity" into trouble, forms which lead them to believe, for instance, that there is no real salvation apart from some "specific" of their own prescription. Campbell's views may indeed be idiosyncratic, his creed may strike some as peculiar, and he himself may be critical of those who fail to share his ideas, but is this a valid reason to bring such monstrous charges against him? No, thought the author of *Candour*; no sectarian creed or watchword, no favorite dogma should hide from us the simplicity of the gospel, namely the revelation of God's character and of God's mercy and goodness as articulated in the life—words and actions—of Jesus. We should therefore "not judge a man who professes to be a Christian by any standard of orthodoxy which is a criterion of man's making—about which men differ individually, and which varies in different ages and countries according to the caprice of the majority."[15]

Robert Story, the minister of the adjoining parish in Rosneath, was another of Campbell's supporters. He it was, wrote Campbell, who "proved a faithful friend in dark and trying times." His son, Robert H. Story (who was to succeed his father as Minister of Rosneath), described the situation at the outbreak of the Row heresy as a "time that was ripe for new expansion and development of Gospel teaching." "The theology of Scotland," he wrote, since it was a theology "raised on so dogmatic a foundation," had "ceased to have much living influence on the popular conscience."[16] Campbell, he went on to say, was sadly aware of the hypocrisy and superficiality of many of his parishioners' religious attitudes, and quotes him as saying:

> I was gradually taught to see that so long as the individual is uncertain of being the object of love to his God, and is still without any sure hold of his personal safety, in the prospect of eternity, it is in vain to attempt to induce him to serve God under the power of any purer motive than the desire to win God's love for himself, and so to secure his own happiness.[17]

If Robert Story was one of the few who voted against Campbell's subsequent deposition, his support, as well as that of a handful of others, did little to stay the inexorable process by which the Kirk sought and obtained the Minister of Row's condemnation. Indeed (wrote William Hanna many years later), "Mr. Campbell needed all the support that could be given. His friends were few, his opponents all-powerful. From almost every leading pulpit he had been denounced ... [Many were the ministers who] vied with one another in expressing through the press their sense of the depth and dangerous nature of the errors into which he had fallen."[18]

CHAPTER THREE: THE ROW HERESY

Campbell's "errors" stemmed, in fact, not from his gift for theological speculation, but from his genuine concern for the spiritual well-being of his parishioners. By his own admission, this initially took two forms. First, upon assuming his responsibilities at Row, he determined to use only the Bible as the sole resource for preparing his sermons. Second, in his parochial visits, he resolved to have his conversation given over entirely to specifically religious concerns and not to limit his "ministerial intercourse" to ecclesial occasions only, since "religion was [for him] a thing truly of all times and of all seasons."

> These two circumstances [he wrote]—my exclusive study of the Word of God, and my exclusive intercourse as the servant of God with man—increased rapidly my acquaintance with the extent of the demands for personal religion on the part of God, and with the little measure of compliance with these on the part of men, and rendered my meditations chiefly researches into the reasonableness of the former, and the consequent sin in not meeting them, and the various devices of Satan by which men were enabled to live at peace in a reasonable way; and my discourses contained the exposition of the discoveries on these subjects, which they were daily making to me, along with such personal warnings, and practical exhortations to my people as these discoveries suggested.[19]

These "discoveries" may at first have been inchoate, but increasingly they crystallized as firm and clearly articulated convictions. But, as his reputation as a preacher grew, so did the suspicion that some, at least, of his views were perhaps unsound (and, as one cleric was to comment later, "to a christian minister there can be no more serious imputation than that of unsoundness!"[20]). News of the Row preaching, especially Campbell's exposition of the "Doctrine of Assurance," soon reached Glasgow, and, in the winter of 1827, Campbell himself went to a meeting of the Glasgow Theological Society to hear an address on "The Assurance of Faith," an address in which he discerned many serious errors. Campbell was invited by his clerical colleagues to respond to the address, which he did (very likely at some length!), but at the time there appear to have been no misgivings as to what he said. Later in the same week, however, Campbell preached "for one of Glasgow's charitable institutions" on the "practical importance" of the Assurance of Faith. Most of the Glasgow clergy attended and "it is from this occasion," wrote Campbell, "that I date the opposition of my breathren," although there was at this time "no organized opposition in the parish of Row."[21] The opposition did, however, grow and, over the next two years both parish and presbytery became involved, particularly as Campbell's preaching on "assurance" led him to express himself in respect to the universality of forgiveness and the limitless extent of the Atonement. Campbell, it is clear, was both saddened and surprised by the tenor of the response to his preaching. Surprised, too, he must have been, that short-hand transcriptions of his sermons were being made, printed, and circulated. There were those, he said, who claimed that "[i]f all are forgiven, then we need not repent, or be sorry for our sins, or think of a future judgment, and we may do as we please." Campbell was indeed "shocked to hear men avow that if they were certain their Heavenly Father forgave them their sin they would feel it unnecessary to grieve [if] they offended Him."[22]

Campbell, then, like Erskine, was to be charged with what many of his contemporaries thought to be the most heinous of theological aberrations, Antinomianism. Eventually, in March of 1830, eight of Campbell's parishioners were persuaded to make a formal charge to the Presbytery. A libel (indictment) was then duly drawn up and signed by these parishioners: 3 farmers, 1 spirit-dealer, 1 grocer, 1 surgeon, and 2 petty tacksmen.[23] Campbell was then directed to preach, from his own pulpit in Row, before an official Presbyterial Visitation. This was in July, and by the following September the case had been heard in court and the libel proven "relevant." The matter was then finally brought before the Synod of Glasgow and Ayr in May of 1831. The libel, in its final form as submitted to the Synod was accurate as to its representation of Campbell's views; it was also clearly indicative as to how his views and those of Erskine converged. It reads in part:

> Mr. John Macleod [sic] Campbell, Minister of the Gospel at Row, You are indicted and accused ... by the subscribers, heads of families, and inhabitants of the said parish, that albeit the doctrine of universal atonement and pardon through the grace of Christ, as also the doctrine that assurance is one of the essence of faith, and necessary to salvation, are contrary to the Holy Scriptures and to the Confession of Faith approven by the General Assemblies of the Church of Scotland ... yet true it is and of a verity, that you the said John McLeod Campbell hold and have repeatedly promulgated the aforesaid doctrines from the pulpit or other place or places from which you have read discourses ... [Y]ou have declared that God has forgiven the sins of all mankind whether they believe it or not: That in consequence of the death of Christ, the sins of every individual of the human race are forgiven; That it is sinful and absurd to pray for an interest in Christ, because all mankind have an interest in Christ already: And that no man is a Christian unless he is positively assured of his salvation.[24]

Many people have remarked on the often vitriolic and uncharitable nature of this long and gloomy judicial procedure. Indeed, in reviewing the Row controversy, one English observer, deploring the "spirit of strife" exhibited by the participants, commented wryly: "All this seems to indicate a degree of excitement and commotion in the religious public north of the Tweed, of which we more phlegmatic English folk can scarcely form an idea."(!)[25] Even the controversial flavor of the many long speeches recorded in *The Whole Proceedings* does not save

CHAPTER THREE: THE ROW HERESY 35

that volume from being tedious in the extreme. Campbell himself spoke in his own defense, and at considerable length. Robert Story's testimony, as well as Thomas Carlyle's arguments, were diffuse and unfocused. The latter's speech lasted for 3 hours and 10 minutes—so it is not surprising that "while Mr. Story and he spoke, [the delegates] went almost all out ... and only returned towards the end of the speaking from the bar."[26]

Two points of interest, however, emerge from the *Proceedings*. First, it was stated, in spite of Campbell's request that he be judged by the light of Scripture and Scripture alone, that the "Standards of the Church" (i.e., The Westminster Confession, &c.) would be the only basis upon which the case would be argued. "Any detailed reference to the Scriptures," it was declared, was "altogether unnecessary." Or, as one clergyman remarked, "We are far from appealing to the Word of God on this ground: it is by the Confession of Faith that we must stand: by it we hold our livings."[27] Second, much was made of the similarity between Campbell's views and those of the Marrowmen. If Chalmers could lightly observe that Erskine's *Unconditional Freeness* might be characterized as the "*Marrow of Modern Divinity* modernised," the Synod was insistent in its pointing out again and again that the Marrow Theology had been condemned in 1720 by the General Assembly of the Church of Scotland; that condemnation was, therefore, one of the "standards" by which Campbell was to be tried.[28]

Tried he was, and condemned. The result was a foregone conclusion. The vote was 119 to 6 against him. The "solemn and deliberate judgment" of the Synod was read by the Moderator:

> In the name of the Lord Jesus Christ, the sole King and Head of His Church, and by virtue of the power committed by him to it, I do now solemnly depose Mr. John M'Leod Campbell, minister of the parish of Row, from the office of the holy ministry, prohibiting and discharging him from exercising the same, or any part thereof, in all time coming, under pain of the highest censure of the church; and I do hereby declare the church and parish of Row vacant from and after the day and date of this sentence.[29]

Upon the reading of this judgment, one amusing incident did take place. The Chief Clerk of the Synod—filled, one supposes with emotion—proclaimed in the hearing of all his agreement with what had just been done but ended up by saying exactly the opposite of what he meant; namely, that "these doctrines of Mr. Campbell would remain and flourish after the Church of Scotland had perished and was forgotten." Upon hearing this, Erskine, who had been in attendance throughout the trial, whispered to those near him: "This spake he not of himself, but being High Priest—he prophesied!"[30]

There was also a poignant note to the affair. Just prior to the vote which condemned Campbell, his father, the Rev. Dr. Donald Campbell of Kilninver rose and read to the assembly a letter signed by more than 400 parishioners from Row. The letter was a palpable testimony to the affection in which Campbell was still held by the members of his parish, in spite of the original libel having its origin there. The father then, after making a plea for "leniency and mercy," concluded by saying, "Moderator, I am not afraid for my son. Though his brethren cast him out, the master whom he serves will not forsake him; and, while I live, I will never be ashamed to be the father of so holy and blameless a son."[31]

The Row heresy trial thus came to an end. Oddly, Thomas Chalmers "preserved unbroken silence"[32] during the conflict, but he did cause to be reprinted Archbishop James Ussher's *A Letter Concerning the Death and Satisfaction of Christ*, originally written in 1617; this he distributed to his divinity students so that they might be better informed on the doctrinal issues then being controverted. But if Chalmers was silent, a host of others, reflecting on Campbell's deposition, were increasingly critical of what had taken place. If Campbell's supporters were, during the trial, few, subsequent to the Synod's action, the pendulum of theological opinion gradually swung in his favor. As Norman Walker has observed, "No thoroughly earnest man was ever long left without followers in those days, and [many were those] who drank of the charmed spring of the Gareloch."[33] D.J. Vaughan has said much the same thing: "The deposed minister of Row,—the man cast out of the Church of Scotland as a heretic five-and-forty years ago,—lived to be honoured by the Church which had cast him out."[34] One instance of an honor bestowed upon Campbell paralleled Erskine's receipt of an honorary degree from the University of Edinburgh. Campbell was similarly honored in 1869 by the University of Glasgow. In response to this signal event, Erskine wrote to Campbell: "I wonder if the Church of Scotland will not at last take the step of reponing you, when the Glasgow University confers the degree of D.D. on you" (Hanna, p. 492). Robert H. Story's testimony in respect to what happened to Campbell is predictably favorable: "The theological thought and teaching to which Mr. Campbell [and Mr. Erskine] gave the first open impulse, and which his deposition did not check or deaden, has perceptibly modified the theology of Scotland ... [It was] Mr. Campbell's destiny to bear the brunt of the first deliberate encounter between the forms of a doctrinal system which, emptied of [its] living meaning, had lost [its] strong hold over men's consciences, and the deeper earnestness and spirituality which met the new wants and aspirations with a new and diviner teaching ... He suffered—but theology gained thereby."[35]

Although not intended as such, Archibald Robertson's epigrammatic commentary on the Row heresy may serve as an accurate characterization of Erskine's and Campbell's views: "Those who embrace the doctrines of Universal Pardon and Assurance have *joy* but not *trembling*."[36] But for Campbell and Erskine, "trembling" was no part of the Gospel. Their views, in fact, were soon to become commonplace within British theology, so much so that it is difficult for a person in the twentieth century to understand the vindictive nature of the attacks made against them. Adam Milroy has summed up the situation this way:

> The opposition to Campbell was remarkable for its intensity and unanimity. The Church had tolerated tenets much more inconsistent with the confession, and when charges had been made against individuals holding erroneous opinions, nothing like the spirit displayed in opposing what was called the "Row heresy" had been excited. But on the only two occasions [the other being the Marrow controversy in 1720] in which universal pardon and assurance came before the church courts, all parties combined in condemning those two heresies with a burning zeal which all other heresies failed to rouse. Moderates and Evangelicals laid aside their differences for a time, and cordially joined in throwing out of the Church one of her most earnest and saintly ministers for teaching that God loved all the children of mankind; that this love was revealed in Christ, who had procured remission of sin for all; and that man's faith in this revelation must be firm and sure.[37]

Further evidence of Campbell's growing reputation is the wide acclaim given him (by F.D. Maurice, among others) upon the publication of his *The Nature of the Atonement*,[38] a volume which "would probably have never seen the light," as one historian has said, "if it had not been for Erskine's earlier writings on the subject."[39] The acclaim given Campbell's volume on the Atonement, however, and the growing acceptance of Erskine and Campbell's doctrinal opinions, has not, it must be said, been universal. As late as 1939, for instance, in a series of lectures given at the Westminster Theological Seminary, John Macleod claimed that Campbell

> resolves the atoning work of our Lord into an adequate repentance such as no one but a sinless Savior could render and bring forward. This view held implicit in its bosom the Deistic teaching that an adequate repentance is the only Atonement that is needed. The penal, the forensic, the judicial aspect of the great transaction is spirited away. It melted into the thinnest of thin air. Campbell's follower [*sic*] and friend, Thomas Erskine of Linlathen, became as an amiable Broad Churchman the centre of a circle of revised Moderatism which, while it claimed to be religious, broke away from the mysteries of the Evangelical Faith. Its engrossing doctrine was that of a Divine Fatherhood which is quite universal ... [T]his fervid hyper-evangelism of the Row teaching burnt itself out and it left not even the ashes of Evangelical Faith behind.[40]

Whatever one makes of the sustained influence of the Row teaching (and, obviously, Mr. Macleod did not make much of it!), it is certain that Thomas Erskine and John McLeod Campbell were drawn throughout the controversy into a deep and lasting friendship, a friendship that would be nurtured over the next forty years (Erskine died in 1870 and Campbell two years later). One charming anecdote depicting the nature of their friendship can be seen in a letter from Campbell to Erskine telling him that he had named his son (born in 1841) Thomas Erskine Campbell. Erskine's response was characteristic:

> May the Good Father bless the parents and the children, and make your Thomas Erskine a better man and a wiser than him after whom he is named. I should be sorry to see myself reproduced entire in any human being; and if I thought the name could effect such a thing, I should positively object to its being imposed on the young immortal; but I have the trust that *the names* into which he is to be baptized, is the name which shall be the mould of his character and the fountain of his spiritual life—the name of the Father, and of the Son, and of the Holy Spirit. (Hanna, pp. 251-2.)

For Erskine and Campbell alike, despite their criticisms of the narrowness of Westminster theology, the Christian was called not to argue about God but to proclaim God's love for all people. Erskine invited his readers, as Campbell had invited his parishioners, to draw close to God and by virtue of such intimacy to become "like God," to become, that is, "partakers of the divine nature."[41] Such generosity of spirit and such breadth of theological perception were neither popular nor common in the Kirk of the 1830s. Indeed, as James Walker has said, there is a fairly wide-spread "allegation that Scotch religion is harsh, austere, gloomy;—a stern and frowning thing, revelling in the dark, dread mysteries of a stern theology."[42] Undoubtedly, Erskine and Campbell did much to disperse this gloom and to brighten the darkness of the "stern theology" which was often associated with the "Standards of the Church," so much so that D.J. Vaughan, some years after the Row controversy, could claim without undue exaggeration that, because of their contributions to British theology, albeit at considerable cost to themselves, there is now "a better day in store for the Church, of which such men as Erskine and Campbell are both the promise and the type."[43] It may therefore not be inappropriate to end this chapter with some relevant excerpts from the sermon preached by Robert H. Story on Sunday, the 22nd of February, 1872, five days after Mr. Campbell's death.

> There are those ... who have believed, through all the depths of their spirits, in a living God, revealing Himself to them, and dealing with them, through a living Mediator; who have so loved that which they saw to be the truth and righteousness of God, that they have been

CHAPTER THREE: THE ROW HERESY 39

able to love men with no restrained portion of the love with which they feel Christ loves them.

[Dr. Campbell], who was with us here but two Sundays ago ... was one who has long been held in reverence by great numbers of the wise and good, far beyond the bounds of our community, and of the Scottish Church ... It is forty-seven years since he was ordained, a young and ardent evangelist, to be minister of the church of Row. There, during six years of a devoted ministry, he moved among his people as a "living epistle" of the Lord Jesus Christ ... to Dr. Campbell the Gospel was not a system fenced with logic, parcelled out into propositions. It was the revelation of a Divine Father's character and will. No one could use logic more skillfully than he: no one could reason with more thorough and impartial apprehension of every side of the argument; but he had got within the circle of the logic, and the orderly definitions, and the elaborated doctrines ... That God was the Father of all; that He loved every human soul "with a love the measure of which was the agony of His own Son;" that He made no choice among His children, selecting some, rejecting others ... this was the outline of the Gospel he preached. To many it was the very Word of Life; to some it was the "rock of offence." Those who called it "heresy" went to the Church Courts with their complaints, and were not discouraged when they went.

After a hurried trial, in which it was not proved that he had contravened its "standards," Mr. Campbell was deposed from the office of the holy ministry within the national Church ... [But] his call to be an apostle had a higher sanction than the orders of any branch of the visible Church, and, feeling this, he did not cease to preach the Gospel.

In him all thought, all feeling were religious. "His conversation was in heaven." Of him, as of his friend Thomas Erskine, who was taken to his rest before him, you felt that his life was "hidden with Christ,"—its closest fellowships were within the veil, its deepest realities were in the unseen.

There are but few who, like Dr. Campbell, have so embodied and expressed in their own life the spirit of Christ's, as to make belief in the great Master easy, and doubt of Him impossible. It is no small addition to the sum of any one's responsibilities to have known such a man, and witnessed such a life.[44]

Notes to Chapter Three

1 In 1870, upon hearing of the death of "my beloved Mr. Erskine," Campbell wrote that his "friendship with him had its commencement forty-three years ago." This would place their first meeting in 1827. J. McL. Campbell, *Reminiscences and Reflections* (London, 1873), p. 44. At least a year earlier, however, in a letter dated 25 February 1826, Campbell wrote that he was reading Erskine's *Internal Evidence*: "I have lately been reading a book which I shall take home with me, 'Erskine's Internal Evidences,' [*sic*] which is the only book with that title which deserves the name." *Ibid.*, p. 16.

2 That "Gareloch" was as often as not misspelled "Gairloch" (the correct name of a village some miles to the north in Wester Ross) was bound to cause some confusion. Mr. James Russel, for instance, complained bitterly that, although he was the Minister of Gairloch, heretical views associated with the southern parish of Gareloch were being attributed to him. He felt, he said, like treating these unwelcome invaders as one would poachers. Robert Burns, a major disputant in the Row controversy, acknowledged this and wrote (albeit without correcting the spelling!): "Be it known to all men by these presents, that the arm of the Clyde called 'the Gairloch,' in Dumbartonshire, is not the same thing with the *parish* called 'Gairloch' in Ross-shire; that 'the Rev. John M. Campbell' is not the same person with the 'Rev. James Russel, Minister of Gairloch'."

3 So John Logan, *The Religious Thought of Thomas Erskine of Linlathen* (New York, 1931), p. 15.

4 E.G. Bewkes is very likely correct in his suggestion that "Campbell was never conscious of any relation or dependence [upon Erskine] even at this period. Many authors have followed one another in assuming a teacher-disciple friendship. This is quite unjustified. The friendship was intimate, full of mutual affection, and it was lifelong, but Erskine is to be thought of as the 'beloved friend,' not the teacher." *Legacy of a Christian Mind* (Philadelphia, 1937), p. 46.

5 Robert Burns, *Reply to a Lay Member of the Church of Scotland* (Paisley, 1830). p. 52.

6 William Hanna, *Memoirs of the Life and Writings of Thomas Chalmers* (New York, 1850-52), Vol. 3, p. 251.

7 H.F. Henderson, *The Religious Controversies of Scotland* (Edinburgh, 1905), p. 148.

8 Drummond & Bulloch, *op. cit.*, p. 195.

9 Robert Burns, *The Gairloch Heresy Tried* (Paisley, 1830), pp. 9-10.

10 Burns, *Reply*, p. 40 (note).

11 *The Eclectic Review* (Third Series), Vol. 4 (July-Dec., 1830), p. 68.

12 J. Leslie, *The "Christian Instructor" Instructed* (Edinburgh, 1830), pp. 1, 5.

13 Anon., *Candour; or an Impartial Examination of the Row Heresy* (Glasgow, 1831), p. 4.

14 *Ibid.*, p. 8

15 *Ibid.*, p. 32 and *passim*.

16 Robert H. Story, *Memoir of the Life of Robert Story* (Cambridge, 1862), pp. 139-41.

17 *Ibid.*, p. 145 and Campbell, *Reminiscences*, p. 18.

CHAPTER THREE: THE ROW HERESY 41

18   Hanna (Vol. 1), p. 132.
19   *Reminiscences*, p. 13.
20   Ralph Wardlaw, *Discourses on the Nature and Extent of the Atonement of Christ* (Glasgow, 1843), p. vii.
21   *Reminiscences*, p. 21.
22   *Ibid.*, pp. 25-6. It was at this time that Campbell understandably wrote, "I am daily more impressed with the awful state of our church." *Ibid.*, p. 28.
23   So Story, *op. cit.*, p. 391. The designation of these men and their occupations differs slightly from the account given in *The Whole Proceedings*; and Campbell, writing many years later, remembers there having been *twelve* parishioners who drew up the libel.
24   *The Whole Proceedings*, p. 16.
25   *The Eclectic Review* (Third Series), Vol. 4 (July-Dec., 1830), p. 62. In his declining years, Campbell was to write a brief essay on "Modern Religious Controversy" in which he deplored "the discordant din of conflicting sects and systems, mutual recriminations, [and] mutual persecutions." To underline his views, Campbell quoted Alexander Pope's well-known couplet: "For modes of faith let graceless zealots fight;/ His can't be wrong whose life is in the right." *Reminiscences*, pp. 257, 262. On the subject of controversy, Ralph Wardlaw's comment (*op. cit.*, p. viii) is also apt: "The love of controversy, apart from the love of truth, is irrational and unchristian. But the love of truth may, and at times must, overcome the aversion to controversy."
26   *Reminiscences*, p. 36.
27   Quoted by Henderson, *Religious Controversies*, p. 154. This suggests that "clerical privilege" may indeed have been one of the unacknowledged issues in the Row heresy.
28   See Bewkes, *op. cit.*, pp. 71-9.
29   *Proceedings*, p. 178.
30   Hanna, p. 106. Campbell's friend Alexander Scott was also deposed for holding views contrary to the Westminster Confession. After the deposition, Campbell asked him, "Could you sign the Confession now?" His answer was "No. The Assembly was right: our doctrine and the Confession are incompatible." *Ibid.*
31   *Proceedings*, p. 176-7.
32   Hanna, *Memoir of Thomas Chalmers*, p. 251.
33   N.L. Walker, *Robert Buchanan* (London, 1877), p. 22.
34   D.J. Vaughan, "Scottish Influence on English Thought," *The Contemporary Review*, Vol. 32 (June, 1878), p. 467.
35   Story, *op. cit.*, pp. 178-81.
36   A. Robertson, *A Vindication of "The Religion of the Land,:* (Edinburgh, 1830), p. 247. In a curious and somewhat amusing note entitled "The Difficulty in Finding a Characteristic Name for the Followers of Mr. Erskine," Robertson suggests that to call them Erskinites or Campbellites would be to give inappropriate significance to either of them. Perhaps, he says, they could be called "Eclectics," since they garner their views from such diverse sources, or even "Stoics," since they are proud and overbearing. Robertson even claims that some of Erskine's followers were Baptists, one of whom was baptized three times (saying he was not

a believer the first two times!). "If so," adds Robertson, "it is not impossible that [Erskine] may become the founder of a new sect, which for distinction's sake, we may call POLLAKIBAPTISTS." *Ibid.*, p. 246.

37   Adam Milrow, "The Doctrine of the Church of Scotland," in R.H. Story (ed.), *The Church of Scotlant: Past and Present* (London, 1895), Vol. 4, p. 288.

38   Published originally in 1856, this work went through several editions and has been reissued, with a superb introduction by Edgar P. Dickie, as recently at 1959. Regarding the treatment given Campbell at Row, Dickie quips: "Nowadays we do not slay our prophets, though theological students tend to say that we make them professors, and the effect is the same" (p. xiv).

39   V. Storr, *The Development of English Theology* (London, 1913), p. 355.

40   John Macleod, *Scottish Theology* (Edinburgh, 1943), p. 258.

41   Cf. 2 Peter 1.4, a verse often quoted by Erskine.

42   James Walker, *the Theology and Theologians of Scotland* (Edinburgh, 1888), p. 157. Pencilled in the margin here, in the National Library of Scotland's copy of this book, is a resounding PERFECTLY TRUE!

43   Vaughan, *op. cit.*, p. 473.

44   R.H. Story, *The Risen Christ* (Glasgow, 1872), *passim*. The writer of the obituary notice in the *Glasgow Herald* of February 28, 1872, commented: "[Campbell's] opinion as to particular points of Christian doctrine many might dispute, but no one could be long in his presence without gaining a deeper insight into the spirit of Christianity."

CHAPTER FOUR: THE "WEST COUNTRY MIRACLES"

At the same time that the Doctors of Divinity were attempting to adjudicate the Row heresy, there arose from across the loch reports of some strange happenings. In the village of Helensburgh, on the western shore of the Gareloch, lived one Mary Campbell (recently moved from Fernicarry), while to the south, across the broad reaches of the Clyde, lived twin brothers, James and George Macdonald. These three persons were to become the principals in what might best be described as a tragic drama, for each of them was pilloried as untruthful, deluded, and deceitful. Such charges arose because Campbell and the Macdonalds were involved (unintentionally, it appears) in healings, prophesies, and a variety of spoken and written utterances. Were these truly the manifestations of the Holy Spirit or not? People took sides, and the tragedy is that the ensuing controversy swirled *around* them, a controversy which seldom considered them as persons with any genuine feelings; attention was directed, rather, to the spectacular nature of the so-called miracles and to whether or not they were genuine. To some, these simple folk were the objects of ridicule, while to others, they became symbols of a new age of religious awakening. Erskine became intensely interested and, rather than speculate on the merits of the case from a distance, he himself went to stay with Mary Campbell and with the Macdonalds on several occasions. In doing so, he became convinced of their sincerity as well as of the authenticity of what came to be known as the "West Country Miracles." As a result of this, he wrote a slim pamphlet entitled *The Gifts of the Spirit*, published in 1830. It is without question the most petulant of Erskine's published works, and its mere 24 pages elicited more than twenty times that amount in angry rejoinders. If, in his previous writings, Erskine had come increasingly to challenge the "Religion of the Land," in *The Gifts of the Spirit* he portrayed Scottish religion as dismally lifeless, its ministers as contenders against God, and their protracted disbelief "as nothing less than a form of atheism" (Gifts, p. 21).

The little book begins simply enough with a seemingly innocent inquiry as to why the spiritual gifts recorded in the New Testament seem no longer to be in evidence. Do not such gifts belong to the church? And, if they are not found in the church, does not the want of them arise out of a want of faith within the church? Then, as the tempo of his argument intensifies, Erskine went on to say: "I cannot conceive that Paul should have been taught by the Holy Spirit to leave on record such a detailed system of rules for the right use of spiritual gifts in the church, if these gifts were to be done away [with] so soon after he had written his Epistles" (Gifts, p. 11). He candidly admitted that, while earlier in his life he might have been "revolted" by such miraculous signs, his conversations with Mary Campbell and with the Macdonalds had assured him of the "genuine miraculous character" of the "remarkable facts which have taken place in the West Country" (Gifts, p. 15). In respect to the outbreak of glossolalia, he wrote: "I have heard many people speak gibberish, but this is not gibberish, it is a decidedly compact language" (p. 16). He concluded by saying that he believed these events to be of God and that only those who know God "merely as an abstraction, or as a bundle of doctrines" would disbelieve. That so many did disbelieve was but an indication, Erskine thought, that Christianity was "at a low ebb among us." These "signs" were not only signs from God, they were also signs of the "end": "Oh Reader, have you oil in your lamp?" (pp. 20f).

The issues, then, which Erskine raised in this pamphlet (and not without some acrimony) were threefold: (1) Do, or should the spiritual gifts recorded in scripture continue to be manifested in the life of the church? (2) Are the "West Country Miracles" genuine? (3) Does the lack of spiritual gifts in our midst, or the failure of so many to believe them when they are manifested, testify to that sad state of affairs in which "men have no objection to a *doctrine*, of which they make themselves judges—but they shrink from a *living God*?" (p. 14). To each of these questions Erskine replied, often with dramatic vigor, in the affirmative. It is no surprise, however, that the majority of his critics did not agree with him. The beginning of this disagreement was signaled by the stalwart *Edinburgh Christian Instructor*: "Reports have come to us, wrote the anonymous author as a footnote to a review of publications on the Row heresy, about the West Country miracles— Into these things we are inquiring, and the result we mean to give, by and by, [will be] in the form of an exposé. All we can say at present is that such insults on our religion and on our common sense, neither deserve, nor shall receive, any quarter."[1] Readers of the *Instructor* did not have long to wait for this promise (threat?) to be fulfilled, for in a short two months the necessary investigations had been made and the verdict was in, a verdict in respect not only to the "miracles" but to Erskine himself: "If ever we had any hope of Mr. Erskine's recovery from delusion, since he speculated and raved on universal pardon and its cognate heresies, they are not gone; for he believes in the gift of tongues having been conferred on certain ship carpenters in Port-Glasgow, and [on] a feverish damsel or two in Dumbartonshire [who] should be pitied for their insane delusions."[2] A more pointed, and equally argumentative, article stated that the miracles recorded in the New Testament were there primarily to be seen as testimony to the divine inspiration of scripture. Miracles, in fact, for all their capacity to elicit alarm or astonishment, are not an essential part of the Christian faith. After all, can that faith have been totally "submerged all these centuries and utterly forsaken" until somehow it was wonderfully possessed by some untutuored Scots in these last days? Miss Campbell and the Macdonalds are undoubtedly "impostors," and Mr. Erskine, it would seem, has been given to believe this "sheer nonsense" with not so much as a "shadow of proof." But, more important, Erskine gives ample evidence of a "lamentable indecorum" in the ways he speaks of God—he employs a most "disgusting familiarity of expression."[3]

The indomitable Archibald Robertson added his voice to the growing chorus of critics with his observation that the "absurd pretensions" of the Gareloch enthusiasts "must soon be laid aside. Even the credulous cannot always be duped.

CHAPTER FOUR: THE "WEST COUNTRY MIRACLES" 45

Pretenders to inspirations and miracles will soon be as contemptible as their names are notorious."[4] But it was Edward Craig, then minister of St. James' Chapel in Edinburgh, who wrote the most thoughtful and sustained critique of Erskine's *The Gifts of the Spirit* and who came closer than any of his more vituperous colleagues to discerning the real nature of the issues at stake. "We stand charged by you [Erskine]," he wrote, "with resisting God's miraculous testimony to his power and nearness, and with doing this, because we shrink from a living, acting God; nay more, you affirm that this results from an atheistical tendency."[5] Craig did not want to impugn the sincerity of Erskine's faith, but he did question why Erskine had so vehemently accused those who failed to perceive in the West Country miracles the hand of God at work, namely, that "body of ministers who have cordially devoted themselves to the service of their master." In sum, Craig believed that Erskine was seeking either to "convert us" or to "crush us."[6] The evidence, he thought, neither supported the genuineness of the "miracles," nor did it justify such sweeping and all-encompassing charges on Erskine's part:

> We want no sign other than such as the record [i.e., scripture] has given us. But if there is to be a sign, let it be in accordance with the glorious working of God in the olden time, and more consentaneous to the powers of judgment which God has bestowed on us ... We cannot receive this scanty, lame, and ill compacted evidence: we reject it as unworthy of the great cause to which we adhere; and while we reject it on such grounds, we do not fear the charge of being heartless, infidel, or atheistical.[7]

The Christian church is indeed "at a low ebb," remarked Craig (repeating Erskine's own phrase), if it has to resort to the "utterance of an unintelligible gabble" to prove its vitality. Has not Mr. Erskine confused "proofs" with mere "opinion," and has he not argued *a priori* that since their *ought* to be miracles, then surely there *must* be? But are not the moral powers derived from a divine truth that is revealed and accepted of far greater importance to the Christian life than the exhibition of strange behavior on the part of a few persons in the West of Scotland who may be as much themselves deceived as they are deceiving of others? "We wait patiently," Craig concluded, "for plain, straightforward, open, unsuspicious evidence of direct and unequivocal miracles before we can give you [Mr. Erskine] our confidence."[8] And then departing only this once from his restrained and irenic tone, Craig added:

> If you ask the multitude to seek confirmation of the truth by miraculous testimony, which is not in the economy of God to vouchsafe, you may impede the simple belief of the gospel testimony; you may confirm the ready scepticism of the natural heart; you may ruin souls; but their blood will be required at your hand.[9]

A less sanguine example of the response to Erskine's *The Gifts of the Spirit* appeared in *The Eclectic Review*, written by an anonymous author (an English cleric?) and giving ample testimony to the remarkably caustic tenor of much of nineteenth-century polemical rhetoric. This writer questioned if "the great facts of Christianity [could be] attested by no better testimony than the fanatical pretensions of the Maid of Fernicarry."[10] He then goes on to say:

> Alas for Thomas Erskine! We have been slow to believe that he too could be the dupe of this new Joanna and her lying miracles ... Mr. Erskine's case is clear,—and we fear hopeless. The narcotic doctrines he has imbibed have induced a paralysis of his reasoning powers ... [We] take leave of Mr. Erskine, with the expression of our sincere though not sanguine hope, that he may yet live to see the true nature of the pernicious delusions which have corrupted his fine mind.[11]

There is no record of Erskine's response to these attacks made upon him; he wrote nothing either in his own defense or in defense of what he had written in *The Gifts of the Spirit*. Yet, ironically, Erskine himself came to distrust the suasive power of miracles, and many of the arguments which Craig and others raised against him he would soon be articulating in his own writing, especially in his letters. Also, over a period of two or three years, he began to question the authenticity of the Helensburg and Port-Glasgow miracles themselves. His initial doubts may have stemmed from his growing suspicion of the undue emphasis placed on the gifts of the Spirit in some quarters, and perhaps especially on that kind of spontaneous revivalism engendered in Edward Irving's newly established "Catholic Apostolic Church" in London. These doubts may also have arisen because he had come to realize that his attempts to relate the wide-spread rejection of the Gareloch miracles to the moribund state of Scottish religion was, after all, a futile exercise, theologically inappropriate, and pragmatically misdirected. In any event, the first indication of Erskine's change of heart was expressed in a letter to Thomas Chalmers, written in May of 1832, a letter which suggests, wrote Hanna, that Erskine's faith in "some at least" of the Port-Glasgow manifestations remained unshaken, implying that others had indeed been called into question (Hanna, p. 139). In the letter itself, Erskine compared the authority of the Westminster Confession with the authority of those gifts whose declared purpose was to edify the church and preserve its unity, never to be the guarantor of doctrine:

> Now, is it a sin of the Church, or only a misfortune, that she is without the gifts [of the Spirit], and therefore obliged to have recourse to a Confession for the purpose of unity? Surely the Westminster divines did not exhaust the Bible; and if they had the Spirit, surely the divines of our day are not excluded from the Spirit,

CHAPTER FOUR: THE "WEST COUNTRY MIRACLES"

> and if so, they ought to thank God for what light was seen before, and press on the further light in the strength of the Spirit. If it be the sin of the Church to be without the gifts, then the necessity of the Confession is a sinful necessity, and ought not to be pleaded against any man who appeals to the Word and the interpretations of the Spirit. (Hanna, p. 141.)

But, apart from this, the question as to whether Mary Campbell and the Macdonald brothers were instruments of God's Spirit still had to be addressed. Were they divinely chosen vessels through whom the church might be renewed, for indeed it was a church drastically in need of renewal? Erskine was surely wrestling with these and similar questions. And soon he began to wonder. Was he mistaken? Had he spoken too presumptuously or decided too prematurely? Yet, even as such doubts entered his mind, never once did he question the integrity or sincerity of those three persons who, because of the nature of the controversy swirling around them, were treated as player-pawns on a much larger stage. Erskine alone, it seems, treated them with both affection and sensitivity. As to his doubts, however, the questions narrowed down to the distinction between "power" and "truth." Miracles, indeed, exert an awesome power, but do they point to the truth? Not always, thought Erskine. By December of 1833, in a letter to his cousin Rachel, he was able to state this unambiguously:

> My mind has undergone a considerable change ... God is our all, and having God, we have lost nothing. These gifts are but signs and means of grace; they are not grounds of confidence; they are not necessarily intercourse with God; they are not holiness, nor love nor patience. They are not Jesus. But surely they shall yet appear, when God has prepared men to receive them ... The true connection of man with the Spirit of God is seeking to know and do his will ... I cannot believe that there has been no outpouring of the Spirit at Port-Glasgow and in London; but I feel that I have to wait in every case upon the Lord, to receive in my heart directly from Himself my warrant to acknowledge anything to be of His supernatural acting, and I have erred in not waiting for this. (Hanna, pp. 150, 152)

The tenor of this statement, as well as its specific implications, suggests that Erskine's certainty in respect to the gifts of the Spirit was waning and that the "powerful" authority of miracles themselves had therefore to give way to the more "truthful" authority of subjective, inner illumination. But even that inner certainty was lacking: "I have not in me a light that confirms ... so neither have I a light which distinctly condemns" (Hanna, p. 152). It is not clear whether this "inner light" was ever vouchsafed Erskine, but it is clear that some objective (albeit unexpected) data concerning the case confirmed his growing suspicions. It was discovered, for instance, that some of the "prophetic utterances" of James Macdonald stemmed not from divine inspiration but from some newspaper articles which he had recently read. And the inspired "writing" of Mary Campbell (thought by some to be Chinese or some African dialect!) was upon inspection (by some Cambridge University dons) discovered to be no "decidedly compact language" at all. A further objective argument, based on the New Testament, was that in every instance of ecstatic speech little or no "interpretation" had been provided. Without such interpretation, if one accepts Paul's admonition in 1 Corinthians 12:27-28, glossolalia is meaningless and absurdly unedifying.

James Macdonald died in 1835, and his brother George a year later. Erskine had attended James' funeral and wrote soon after to Rachel that he had been a man "convinced that the voice which spoke by him was the voice of the Spirit ... James ... was an amiable man and [a] clean character—perfectly true. And those manifestations which I so often witnessed in him were indeed most wonderful things and most mighty, and yet—I am thoroughly persuaded—delusive" (Hanna, pp. 165f). Then later, in 1837, Erskine first made public in writing his sad recognition that both he and those who were the principals in the West Country miracles had indeed been subject to delusion. In a note appended to his *The Doctrine of Election*, published that year, he confessed that that much of what he had written earlier in *The Gifts of the Spirit* and in *The Brazen Serpent*[12] were things which he no longer believed:

> In two former publications of mine ... I have expressed my conviction that the remarkable manifestations which I witnessed in certain individuals in the West of Scotland about eight years ago were the miraculous gifts of the Spirit, of the same character as those of which we read in the New Testament. Since then, however, I have come to think differently, and I do not now believe they were so. But I still continue to think that to anyone whose expectations are formed by, and founded on, the declarations of the New Testament, the disappearance of these gifts from the Church must be a greater difficulty than their re-appearance could possibly be. I think it but just to add, that though I no longer believe those manifestations were the gifts of the Spirit, my doubts as to their nature have not at all arisen from my discovery, or even suspicion, of imposture in the individuals in whom they have appeared. On the contrary, I can bear testimony that I have not often in the course of my life met with men more marked by native simplicity and truth of character, as well as by godliness, then James and George Macdonald, the first two in whom I witnessed these manifestations.

CHAPTER FOUR: THE "WEST COUNTRY MIRACLES"

> Both these men are now dead, and they continued, I know, to their dying hour, in the confident belief that the work in them was of the Holy Ghost. I mention this for the information of the reader who may feel interested in their history, although it is a fact which does not influence my own conviction on the subject.
>
> To some it may appear as if I were assuming an importance to myself in publishing my change of opinion, but I am in truth only clearing my conscience, which requires me thus publicly to withdraw a testimony which I had publicly given, when I no longer believe it myself. (Election, p. 571)[13]

Erskine's *The Doctrine of Election* did not attract as much attention as had his previously published books, and the reviews of it are few. This lack of attention may have been due to its being what Henry Henderson called the only "prolix" work which Erskine wrote.[14] Certainly it has a prolix title![15] In that this book seriously challenged the prevailing (Calvinistic) view of election, it was no less potentially controversial as Erskine's earlier works; indeed, one reviewer noted that the "author has been driven to the necessity of devising an entirely new scheme" which is diametrically opposed to the "common doctrine,"[16] but this was something of which Erskine was already aware. Of the reviews that were published, however, only one (to my knowledge) comments on Erskine's "retraction," and comments quite sympathetically. Some of Erskine's earlier treatises, the anonymous reviewer wrote,

> indicate a strong and settled belief in the miracles said to have been performed in the North, and even in in the supernatural gift of tongues. But a more dispassionate study of the principles and facts to which he formerly yielded his conviction, has satisfied him that he was deceived, and accordingly, with that candour and love of truth which seem to pervade all the feeling of his heart, he now acknowledges that he had allowed himself to be misled, or, at all events, to adopt conclusions that his maturer thoughts refuse to sanction.[17]

That the so-called "Row heresy" and the controversies arising out of the West Country miracles occupied Erskine's attention at the same time may indicate that they were not, in his mind at least, disconnected. It was possible, as Duncan Finlayson has suggested, that the vehement attacks made upon John McLeod Campbell (and also upon Alexander Scott, who was also deposed for holding views similar to those of Erskine and Campbell) were perceived as signs of an apocalyptic nature, as signs, that is, of that final catastrophic time when history will be brought to its climactic conclusion.[18] That these attacks were made by ordained ministers in a church whose faith was seen to be so laden with the need to espouse narrow doctrinal orthodoxy that it ended up by portraying a God whose primary attitude towards humankind was one of punitive judgment—this also must have had a profound effect on Erskine's sensibilities. It may therefore have appeared to him as only natural that there would be other "signs of the times," and those signs were indeed forthcoming in the persons of Mary Campbell and James and George Macdonald. If these things were for Erskine "all of a piece," may it not be that his subsequent discovery that they were indeed *not* all of a piece that led him (1) to retract his assertion as to the genuineness of the West Country miracles, (2) to withdraw from theological and ecclesiastical controversies (at least within the public arena), and (3) to soften the tone of his sometimes harsh apocalyptic proclamations. Neither miracles nor controversy nor dire threatenings as to the "end-time" were to find any enduring space within the wider scope of Erskine's theology. Even some seven years after his formal published retraction, Erskine could write (to M. Vinet):

> I am very thankful that you have got any good out of the "Brazen Serpent." During the time that I wrote it I was conscious of communion with God in my own spirit; and whether the view which I take of the history be just or not, I believe that it contains much of the meaning of Christianity. I think that I was mistaken in my impression as to the appearances of spiritual gifts; but that is of very little consequence, and perhaps my chief error in the book is that I give too much importance to them. (Hanna, p. 277)

If Erskine was thus able to look back on the uproar caused by the publication of his *The Gifts of the Spirit* which such seeming detachment, it is hard to believe that the tumultuous events of the 1830s did not take their toll on him; he cannot have been unaffected by the attacks made upon him nor dispassionate in respect to the charges he had laid upon the religious establishment. Did he sense, one wonders, that his advocacy for a "living God" had been blunted by his becoming embroiled in doctrinal issues that were beyond his capacity to articulate them persuasively or that the weight of Westminster orthodoxy was so oppressive that he came to realize the futility of his attempt to bring about the religious and theological reforms which he had so earnestly sought? It would appear that, for all his efforts to bring about change, Erskine was constitutionally neither a "self-conscious innovator" nor a "leader of a movement."[19] Yet whether or not one is able to spy them out with any accuracy, surely there were reasons—internal and external— which led Erskine to give up his writing and to retire from active participation in the theological enterprise. After 1837 no more books were forthcoming from Erskine's pen until the posthumous publication of a few incidental papers gathered together under the title *The Spiritual Order*. Henderson, among others, has admitted that it is difficult to account for these years of silence. "It may be," he wrote, "that his still small voice was hushed to silence, by reason of the ecclesiastical clamour that was thundering around him."[20] Yet surely more than this was involved, as many of Erskine's letters suggest. There is, for instance, clear evidence that he harbored

CHAPTER FOUR: THE "WEST COUNTRY MIRACLES" 51

some self-doubts about his own writings in general, not just in respect to his views on miracles. Aware, for instance, that much of what he had written in *The Doctrine of Election* was "in direct opposition to the received views of Christianity," he admitted, in a letter to his sister Christian (Mrs. Charles) Stirling that he had found it difficult to say what he had wanted to say "without giving more offence than necessary." And of the book itself he wrote: "I am afraid that it will have many great faults as a work. It is deficient in arrangement and proportion; which will make it drag in the reading, to all except those who are really interested in the subject" (Hanna, pp. 182f). Then later, in a letter to his other sister, Davie (Mrs. James) Paterson, he wrote that he wished "to rewrite the book, to make it more compact and more orderly" (Hanna, p. 228), but just a few months earlier he had told his cousin Rachel that Thomas Chalmers had "completely misunderstood" the book, adding somewhat poignantly that he did not "think of writing another book to explain the book which [he had] already written" (Hanna, p. 219).[21]

Erskine's apparent dissatisfaction with his own books can also be seen in a conversation recorded by Principal Shairp:

> Ten years after the publication of the "Doctrine of Election," two distinguished Americans called upon Mr. Erskine, giving as their apology for intruding without introduction their strong desire to become personally acquainted with an author whose writings had made a wide and deep impression on their countrymen. "It is strange," said Mr. Erskine, "it is a long time since I have read any of them." His interviewers named one of his volumes as to which they fancied he could have no such feeling. "My impression is," was the reply, "that that is the one that I would particularly dislike." Cherishing for a time this feeling, Mr. Erskine suffered his earlier publications to go out of print. (Hanna, p. 573)[22]

Similarly, when urged in September of 1844 by Wright Matthews to have his "Introduction" to *Extracts of Letters to a Christian Friend by a Lady* republished, Erskine demurred: "I don't wish to oppose your desire to have that little Essay printed, and yet I know that I could not put my seal to it as I could have done when it was written, and I don't like to put anything forth as the Gospel which contains so imperfect a view of the truth as that little essay does" (Hanna, p. 573). And in a letter written a month later, again to Matthews:

> You are very welcome to do what you please with my books, only don't touch much on the last ... In the introduction to the old lady's letter I remember some severe words about the leprosy of the Church of Scotland which ought to be omitted as hurting without healing ... [T]here are so many things stated there as whole truths

which are only half truths. This is my general fault to them. (Hanna, p. 574).

Such statements on Erskine's part cannot be due solely to false modesty for such ingenuousness was not consonant with his character. His dissatisfaction with much that he had written seems, given these quotations, honest enough, as does his statement that he would like one day to be able to write something "which may contain all the truth I have published, and omit the trash" (Hanna, p. 574). Erskine's self-doubts concerning the effectiveness of his writings to bear testimony to the truth can be seen in his own self-appraisal as to the effectiveness of his own life. One among many such instances is in a letter (6 February 1839) to his Swiss friend, Madame Vinet:

> What a fearful difference between what we ought to be and what we are! Our calling is to be like Christ; filled with the spirit of Christ; uttering in our words and actions the mind of God; and what are we? Alas! I know for myself how little of all that is accomplished in me; and how little the witness which my mouth gives for God's truth is supported by living holiness in my inward and outward history. (Hanna, p. 234)[23]

It would appear, then, that the reasons for Erskine's withdrawal from the public arena were as ultimately unfathomable as they were manifold. Certainly he found himself changing his mind on issues to which he had been previously passionately committed. Too, he gave voice to a growing dislike for the tenor of much of what he had written. And, further, for all his published challenges to the Kirk and its doctrine, he was a person not given temperamentally to controversy. Yet it is impossible, beyond this, to discern the extent to which the many attacks upon him from 1822 onwards played a role in his decision to forego his active life as a "theological heresiarch" and return to his duties at Linlathen as an "exemplary laird."[24] William Hanna is therefore most likely at least partially accurate in his assessment:

> The twenty years of Mr. Erskine's life from 1840 to 1860 were in striking contrast to those immediately preceding. From 1828 till 1840 pamphlet after pamphlet, volume after volume, was published; meetings were held, addresses were delivered, means of all kinds, public and private, employed for the dissemination of his favourite ideas. On his return from the Continent in 1840 all this was changed ... It was not that his thoughts were less intently occupied with the great truths of Christianity, or that his faith in them had failed; it was not that the ardent desire to have those forms and aspects of these truths in which they presented themselves to his own mind

CHAPTER FOUR: THE "WEST COUNTRY MIRACLES" 53

welcomed by others had in any way abated. But it does look as if his experience had satisfied him that it was not in the direction either of controversy or outward activities of any kind that his strength could be best employed—as if his hopes of influencing thereby the opinion or action of the Churches had collapsed—as if he had lost heart even for the quieter method of speaking through the press. (Hanna, p. 244)

The years after the publication of *The Doctrine of Election* have been called the "silent years," years in which Erskine cultivated friendships both at home and abroad and years in which, as his published letters indicate, he corresponded with a wide variety of people. Hanna has claimed, somewhat generously, that after Erskine "relinquished public life," there was opened to him a "far more varied sphere of intercourse and correspondence ... especially with some remarkable men of the highest literary ability, and with ideas and sentiments congenial to his own" (Hanna, p. 245). (One needs to add that many of these "remarkable" people were also *women*!) To whatever extent Erskine's influence did or did not increase, one discovers in reading his letters that Erskine either chose not to comment upon, or was for some reason disinterested in, the turbulent events, religious as well as secular, of the mid-and late-nineteenth century. As one observer has noted, "Through the years most throbbing with life of all this century [Erskine] was silent. his silence marks a remarkable [*sic*] indifference to personal fame, perhaps it also marks a want of sympathy with the great pulsations of national life as remarkable in a different direction.[25] There are, for instance, but a few desultory references, in Erskine's letters, to the great Disruption of the Scottish Kirk in 1843 that gave birth to the Free Church of Scotland ("I did not feel myself called to take any part in this movement" [Hanna, p. 273]). He has a few not very positive remarks to make about the Tractarian Movement in the Church of England (They "are so impressed with the evil of setting up the right judgment too much that they would forbid private judgment altogether, and place religion in submission and obedience merely" [Hanna, pp. 246f]). He commented somewhat wryly on the growth of missionary societies (hoping that missionaries "might not weary themselves by attempting to displace one set of dogmas and substitute another"[Hanna, p. 334]). He reacted strongly and scornfully to the publication of Joseph Ernest Renan's *La vie de Jésus* ("Love is to Renan an object of tasteful admiration, not the one great spiritual power in the universe" [Hanna, p. 346]),[26] and even more strongly to the news that David Friedrich Strauss, author of the "scandalous" *Leben Jesu*, had been elected to a Professorship of Theology at the University of Zürich (Hanna, p. 235), a post in fact which Strauss never assumed. Erskine also had some bittersweet observations in respect to the rise of biblical criticism as exemplified by the publication in 1860 of *Essays and Reviews* and the appearance a few years later of Bishop John William Colenso's *The Pentateuch and the Book of Joshua Historically Examined* ("I am prepared to hear any criticisms on [the Bible]; they do not trouble me in the least" [Hanna, p. 404]). And throughout the whole of this correspondence there is but one comment upon Darwin's theory of evolution ("I have no belief in the progress of the species" [Hanna, p. 363]). Beyond these and similar examples, however, Erskine's letters do indeed suggest that his personal preference, after the years of public controversy, was to be "in the world but not of it."[27]

If Erskine's retirement was marked by a seeming lack of interest in national and international affairs, it is also true that his criticisms of the Kirk and its doctrines became muted; the criticisms were still there ("The technical conventionalities of our Scotch preaching seem to me to stifle all the religious life and sentiment of the country" [Hanna, p. 285]), but they were less pointed and less splenetic. But what these letters do show—and herein lies their paramount value—is that Erskine's theological perceptions were undergoing a profound change. This was not so much a matter of "changing his mind" (as with the West Country miracles) as it was a process of deepening and simplifying those convictions which are indeed to be found in his previously published works but now come to the surface articulated with a profound commitment to the truth that is unhampered by the turmoil of controversy in which they originally appeared.[28] His theological views were expressed, in these later years, more as an invitation and less as a challenge, more as a personal testimony and less as an exercise in proving himself right and his detractors wrong. The specifically theological issues he addressed were fewer, and they are addressed more directly. The wheat, as it were, was being separated from the chaff. To this extent, both his letters from 1840 to 1870, as well as the essays collected in *The Spiritual Order*, become a commentary on the books he published between 1820 and 1837. For all his dissatisfaction with much of what he had written, and for all his "retraction" of published views previously held, Erskine's influence did not wane, in spite of his withdrawal from public life. His books were in fact being read by an increasingly appreciative number of people, perhaps more in England and on the Continent than in Scotland, and his circle of friends were to be further instruments of that influence in what they wrote and spoke about him. And when Erskine died, it was clear from the many published notices and reviews that his theological contributions would not die with him.

When Erskine was 17 or 18 years of age he read an essay by John Foster, an English Baptist clergyman, entitled "On a Man's Writing Memoirs of Himself." Remembering this many years later (1845), he wrote, "I determined also to keep a journal of my own history, but gave it up, feeling that I did not do it *truly*" (Hanna, p. 279). It may be that the vicious attacks made upon him by Andrew Thomson, Archibald Robertson, and others, planted in him the suspicion that he had not in his books written as "truly" as he would have liked. Since we do not have the "journal of [his] own history," we cannot tell. But his letters, I would suggest, are not unlike a journal in that they provide the reader with intimate glimpses of Erskine's evolving thought while at the same time giving clear evidence that what he wrote in these later years grew directly and "truly" out of what he had written earlier.

Erskine had indeed, by his own admission, been subject to interpretive extravagance in his belief as to the West Country miracles, for instance, but he did not give up his belief in miracles. They were no longer for him seen as signs of the end nor the lack of them a sure indication of the sickness of the Kirk; no more did he speak of the "power" of miracles to impress, convince, or sway. Rather, he could place his view of miracles in close connection with his perception of the "history of God" as revealed in scripture. This can be seen in a letter he wrote in 1861 to his good friend Bishop Alexander Ewing:

> I feel that a miraculous previous history, such as that of the Jews, according to the Old Testament record, is required as the preparation for the appearance of Jesus Christ ... Does not a miraculous dispensation seem the reasonable and necessary concomitant of that wonderful light shining in the midst of gross darkness? God thus taught the people that they were not to be slaves of matter, but to be the free children of Him who governs all things. The miracles of the Bible are not marvels, but illustrations of the character of God. (Hanna, pp. 406f)

It was surely Erskine's conviction as to the "character of God" that lay at the heart of his theology, a theology based on his (albeit idiosyncratic) reading of scripture and largely uninformed by those doctrinal and historical issues which belong to the formal training given in a divinity curriculum. Yet unquestionably, Erskine's abiding belief in God's "inextinguishable love," even when it brought him into conflict with the reigning orthodoxy of the day, was a major contributing factor in the progressive liberalization of British theology. It is of course easy to overemphasize Erskine's influence or to resort to excessive hyperbole, as for instance one reviewer of Erskine's letters has done: "Mr. Erskine, indeed, inaugurated a method of inquiry which is more radically affecting theological thought than even the Theses of Luther himself. Luther's quarrel with Rome was one of *degree* ... Erskine's [with the orthodoxy of his day] was one of *kind*.[29] Happily more moderate assessments of Erskine's importance are to be found, one example of which appeared soon after his death:

> [By virtue of Erskine's teaching] the dark thought which some of us can remember, perhaps, as overshadowing our childhood, that in some region of the spiritual world there exists a prison for those whom God has abandoned to the consequences of their sins, has passed away. Orthodoxy no longer demands of us that we believe in an endless Hell, and no one who has for even a moment groaned

[at] the thought that hope ended with the grave will think any price too great for such a gain.[30]

Erskine's views were indeed, for his time, radical, but only because he knew that the Gospel of God's love was radical beyond human imagining. Much of what he wrote was naïve and on occasion ill-considered; his passion for the truth at times led him to unfortunate excesses of expression; there are even palpable inconsistencies to be found in his books and letters. Yet, underlying all this was a theological vision which gifted the religious and theological world with a new hope and a new confidence. It is to an examination and interpretation of this theological vision and the contours of Erskine's "new" orthodoxy that the following chapters are devoted.

Notes to Chapter Four

[1] Anonymous, "Review of Publications in the Row Heresy," *Edinburgh Christian Instructor*, vol. 29, no. 5 (May, 1830), p. 352.

[2] Anonymous, "Review of a Vindication...," *Edinburgh Christian Instructor*, vol. 29, no. 7 (July, 1830), pp. 502f.

[3] Anonymous, *The Port-Glasgow Miracles* (Hamburg, 1830), *passim*.

[4] Robertson, *op. cit.*, p. 302.

[5] Edward Craig, *A Letter to Thomas Erskine* (Edinburgh, 1830), p. 4.

[6] *Ibid.*, p. 5.

[7] *Ibid.*, p. 12.

[8] *Ibid.*, p. 41.

[9] *Ibid.*, p. 45.

[10] Review of Erskine, *The Gifts of the Spirit*, in *The Eclectic Review*, third Series, vol. 4 (July-Dec., 1830), p. 417.

[11] *Ibid.*, p. 20-24.

[12] Published in 1831, with the sub-title *Life Coming Through Death*, this is clearly the most theologically significant of Erskine's books. In subsequent editions he saw that specific passages dealing with spiritual gifts or expressing apocalyptic fervor were deleted.

[13] Was it intentional or merely an oversight which led Erskine in his "retraction" to mention James and George Macdonald, but not Mary Campbell, by name?

[14] Henry F. Henderson, *Erskine of Linlathen*, p. 36.

[15] See bibliography.

[16] Review of *The Doctrine of Election* in *The Eclectic Review*, New Series (*bis*), vol. 4 (July-Dec., 1838), pp. 101,103.

[17] Review of *The Doctrine of Election* in *The British Critic, and Quarterly Theological Review*, vol. 23 (1838), pp. 320f.

CHAPTER FOUR: THE "WEST COUNTRY MIRACLES" 57

[18] Duncan Finlayson, "Aspects of the Life and Influence of Thomas Erskine of Linlathen, 1788-1870," *Records of Scottish Church History Society*, vol. 20, pt. 1 (1978), p. 39.

[19] So Steve Gowler, "No Second-hand Religion," *Church History*, vol. 54, no. 2 (June, 1985), p. 202.

[20] Henderson, *op. cit.*, p. 40.

[21] See also Hanna (p. 217): "I often feel discouraged from expressing my thoughts, by finding that I do it in so imperfect a manner as to give an entirely false impression of them."

[22] See Finlayson's description of this conversation, p. 45.

[23] It was Mme. Vinet's husband Alexandre who would write Erskine an appreciative note concerning *The Brazen Serpent*: Laissez-moi vous dire combien je dois à un livre qui vient de vous, quoique vous ne me l'ayez pas envoyé: 'The Brazen Serpent. (Le serpent d'airain)' que de choses qu'il me semble avoir toujours pensées! Oh! s'il m'était donneé de sentir avec vous comme il m'a été donné de penser avec vous!" (Hanna, pp. 275f)

[24] The terms are those of the anonymous reviewer of Hanna's "The Letters of Thomas Erskine" (vol. 2) in *The Spectator* (Dec. 29, 1877), p. 1661.

[25] Review of "Mr. Erskine's Posthumous Fragments" [*The Spiritual Order*], *The Spectator* (July 14, 1871), p. 768.

[26] In the first essay in *The Spiritual Order* Erskine's comments on Renan's *Vie de Jésus* are further elaborated.

[27] So, too, Julia Wedgwood: "[Erskine's] life recurs to one's memory like the sigh of an exile. He never took root in this world." Thomas Erskine of Linlathen," in *Nineteenth Century Teachers and Other Essays* (London: Hodder and Stoughton, 1909), p. 75.

[28] John B. Logan has rightly observed: The clearest evidence of Erskine's influence is contained in his letters...[They] remained popular religious reading for many years and still [offer] the best impression of the man and his teaching." Thomas Erskine of Linlathen: Lay Theologian," *Scottish Journal of Theology*, vol. 37 (1984), p. 36.

[29] Review of Hanna, "The Letters of Thomas Erskine" (vol. 1), *The Spectator* (June 23, 1877), p. 794. One is reminded of Thomas Hughes' equally extravagant statement about F.D. Maurice: "The world has only had three great theologians, Augustine, Luther, and Maurice, and the greatest of these is Maurice." Quoted by W.M. Davies, *An Introduction to F.D. Maurice's Theology* (London: SPCK, 1964), p. 1.

[30] *The Spectator* (June 24, 1871), p. 769.

CHAPTER FIVE: BIBLICAL AUTHORITY

> If any textual emendations or any improved translations [of Scripture] could bring the truth [of God's revelation] to light, I should welcome them with my whole heart. (Hanna, p. 404)

It has already been noted that when John McLeod Campbell was tried for heresy, it was by the "Standards" of the Kirk (i.e., the Westminster Confession and the Longer and Shorter Catechisms), and not by Scripture, that he was to be judged. And it was by those very Standards that he was found to have strayed from strict orthodoxy. His condemnation was therefore not unexpected; it was in fact a foregone conclusion. The irony of this is that the Westminster Confession itself assigns primary, if not exclusive, authority to Scripture:

> Although the light of nature, and the works of creation and providence, do so far manifest the goodness, wisdom, and power of God, as to leave no men inexcusable, yet are they not sufficient to give that knowledge of God, and of his will, which is necessary unto salvation; there it pleased the Lord...to reveal himself, and to declare that his will unto his Church; and afterwards, for the better preserving and propagating of the truth...to commit the same unto writing; which maketh the holy Scripture to be the most necessary; those former ways of God revealing his will unto his people being now ceased.[1]

The Confession goes on to assert God as the "Author" of Scripture and that only in Scripture are contained those things without belief in which no one can be saved. Further, "the infallible rule of interpretation," the Confession adds, "is the Scripture itself." That Campbell was tried by the Standards, in spite of what the Standards said about Scripture, may have been because of the famous "formula of 1711" (originally intended to exclude from the ordained ministry those who had Jacobite or Episcopalian sympathies) to which all ministers of the Kirk had to subscribe:

> I do hereby declare that I do solemnly own and believe the whole doctrine contained in the Confession of Faith...to be the truths of God: and I do own the same as the confession of my faith.[2]

For Thomas Erskine, however (as, in fact, for Campbell as well), there was no question but that Scripture, and not creeds or confessions, was the surest and most reliable source for religious knowledge and the paramount point of reference for the living of a Christian life. Many of his published writings were in large part expositions of biblical themes or biblical passages, while throughout his letters there are constant references or allusions to biblical texts. Erskine's intimate knowledge and frequent use of Scripture has led one commentator to state (even while inserting his own biblical allusion!): [One is] amazed at Erskine's ability to live, and move, and have his being in the 'ipsissima verba' of Scripture."[3]

It would appear at first glance that, at least initially, the Bible was an exclusive or even inerrant source of authority for Erskine, or that he subscribed to the then widely held doctrine of verbal inspiration. This is especially true of much of what he wrote in *Internal Evidence*. It is in that volume that he several times expressed his belief that the Holy Spirit "is represented as dictating originally the revealed word, and is still waiting and assisting its progress. He is where the truth is." More than this, "the Spirit never acts except through the medium of the doctrines of the bible" (Evidence, p. 100). And it is these very doctrines which unquestionably indicate the Bible's authenticity: "[W]e need no other testimony" (Evidence, p. 14). Biblical doctrines, that is, are to be distinguished from those other doctrines which have their source or context other than in Scripture. It is clear that Erskine was (and continued to be) displeased with those who, as he saw it, derived their religious views from "creeds and church articles,"[4] since in them God's saving grace is not made "to stand forth with its real prominency" (Evidence, p. 61). Creeds and church articles, he said, are but "Tests and summaries" which, historically

> originated from the introduction of doctrinal errors and metaphysical speculations into religion, and, in consequence of this, they are not so much intended to be the repositories of truth as barriers against the encroachment of erroneous opinions. The doctrines contained in them therefore are not stated with any reference to their real object in the Bible,--the regeneration of the human heart...They appear as detached propositions, indicating no moral cause, and pointing to no moral effect. (Evidence, pp. 62f)

Since the Bible is the "only perfectly pure source of Divine knowledge" (Evidence, p. 93), it was initially Erskine's view that any other form of doctrinal articulation, however prominent, served more to defend a particular point of view or ideology than to teach true religion; more, therefore, to obscure and perplex than to enlighten. In fact, he believed that a person who derives his or her views from sources other than Scripture risks losing even what value there might be in such sources. More than a few times he criticized the "unaccountable and most unfortunate propensity" to look for religious information anywhere other than in the Old and New Testaments (Evidence, p. 78), and that "anywhere" referred not only to creeds and confessions but to a variety of other approaches to Christian doctrine as well, including what he constantly pilloried as "scholastic metaphysics" (Faith, p. 9, &c). The *use* to which such extra-biblical doctrines was put could be as "perverted" as their *content* unilluminating.

CHAPTER FIVE: BIBLICAL AUTHORITY 61

> I cannot but think [wrote Erskine] that the time-honoured use of creeds in which all the articles of belief are crowded together without the smallest indication of their purpose, must have a very questionable tendency for many minds; especially when the idea is suggested, as in the Athanasian Creed, that there is a merit in our believing that which to our reason seems incredible, and that our believing dogmas is the arbitrary condition on which God will bestow on us eternal life. (Sp. Order, p. 16)[5]

Of the many approaches to Scripture which Erskine criticized, it is "dogmatics" that came in for frequent censure. He wrote, for instance, of those "schemes and systems and controversies" which lead a person away from biblical truth. He pointed also to the danger of reading Scripture "with a mind stiffened by dogmatic theology" (Sp. order, p. 104; cf. Evidence, p. 93). Erskine was even more suspicious of those who derived their religious beliefs from 'ecclesiastical polity" rather than from the Bible. Then there are those who relied on their own scholarly erudition rather than on the "simplicity of truth." Concerning these Erskine had this pointed observation to make: "There is not in the world a thing more hateful than to see the Gospel of Jesus Christ converted into an ambitious piece of scholarship" (Faith, p. 100).

For all Erskine's apparent emphasis on the Bible as the exclusive depository of Christian truth, for all his insistence on the sole primacy of scriptural authority and inspiration (i.e., that "the belief of the Gospel is, in every instance, the work of the Holy Spirit, no one who believes in the Bible can doubt" [Evidence, p. 103]), and for all his intimate knowledge of Hebrew and Christian scriptures, Erskine, it turns out, was no biblicist. Indeed he continued to see Scripture as the point of departure for his own theological views, but some of his views went beyond Scripture. And one of those theological views that went beyond Scripture was his understanding of Scripture itself, perceived no longer as the verbally inerrant dictations of the Spirit but as the truly inspired book which served, among other things, to point beyond itself and its own objective authority. Nevertheless, in his earlier writings it is clear that Erskine hesitated to abandon his adherence to the "doctrine" of *Sola Scriptura* or in any way compromise his view of Scripture as the only faithful yardstick by which to assess the truth of a doctrinal assertion. In the last paragraph of his *Unconditional Freeness*, for instance, Erskine made this palpably conciliatory statement:

> I trust [that what] I have written may not do you the injury of exciting the spirit in you of controversy. If you don't agree with it, lay it down and go the Bible; and if you do agree with it, in like manner lay it down and go to the bible, and go in the spirit of prayer

to Him whose word the Bible is, and ask of Him, and He will lead
you into all truth--He will give you living water. (Freeness, p. 159)

That Erskine's writings did indeed excite in many the spirit of controversy has already been well documented,[6] as have the numerous charges made against him, among which was the accusation that he used biblical texts to suit his own purposes, i.e., to make them say what he wanted them to say. Yet Erskine did time and again, even as he began to moderate his understanding of the authority of Scripture (and, it might be added, of authority itself), "go to the Bible," for it was there that he found as nowhere else the history of God's dealings with humankind; there as nowhere else he found the clearest revelation of God's character and of the human condition. The Bible is therefore *our* history too! The Bible, he said, "is the history of God's inward dealings with man's heart; and we can only rightly understand it when we find our personal history in it" (Election, p. 299). "Going to the Bible," then, meant not going to isolated texts to support one's views; it meant, rather, the deep, personal attempt to discern the message of the Bible as a whole, while at the same time discerning how the various parts of the Bible were related to each other. Because he sought faithfully to do this himself, he gradually came to realize that, although the Bible was "inspired," not all parts of the Bible were equally inspired. "[A] spiritual man," he said, "has only true faith in that part of the bible in which he sees and receives God" (Hanna, p. 162). As to the question of inspiration, Erskine did indeed quote the familiar passage from 2 Timothy 3:16 ("All Scripture is given by inspiration of God, and is profitable for doctrine, for reproof, for correction in righteousness"),[7] but he then went on to say (perhaps recalling Richard Hooker) that "there are some passages which, in an especial manner, serve to unfold the mysteries of the Kingdom of God, by setting them before us in their very elements" (Serpent, p. 1). Erskine's assertion as to the multivalent portions of Scripture is clearly illustrated by his observation that "[t]he most zealous defenders of the verbal inspiration of the Bible admit that there are parts of it of less importance than others. This is a great admission, because another is involved in it, namely that we ourselves must be judges of the comparative importance of these different parts" (Sp. Order, p. 85).

Inspiration was for Erskine less a statement as to *how* the Bible got written than a conviction as to *why* it got written.[8] What in fact was the purpose of Scripture and (perhaps more important) what *divine* purpose could be ascertained in Scripture, these were questions of extreme importance. What, that is, is it that "can only be learned by the study of the bBible itself?" "Let [us] but give [our] unprejudiced attention to this book, and [we] will discover that there is contained in it the development of a mighty scheme, admirably fitted for the accomplishment of a mighty purpose" (Evidence, p. 123). So, when through Scripture God reveals to human consciousness (and conscience) glimpses of the divine character, and when human consciousness (and conscience) is thereby influenced and changed, therein lies the true phenomenon of inspiration--not in what the Bible says but in the mutual commerce between God's revelation and human response. Abstract views as to the character of God, if drawn only from a close observation of nature, are less than helpful; it is in the "narration" presented to us in Scripture where

> a most interesting series of actions in which [God's] moral character...is fully and perspicuously embodied. In this narration, the most condescending and affecting and entreating kindness is so wonderfully combined with the most spotless holiness, and the natural appeals which emanate from every part of it, to our esteem, our gratitude, our shame, and our interest, are so urgent and constraining that he who carries about with him the conviction of the truth and reality of his history, possesses in it a principle of mighty efficiency which must subdue and harmonize his mind to the will of that Great Being whose character is there depicted. (Evidence, p. 30)

It is important to note here that the "principles" discerned in the scriptural narration were for Erskine more important than the "events" so narrated.[9] Events in and of themselves may indeed be suasive in their impression on us, but it is the eternal meaning inherent in such events that produce the greater effect. The Atonement, for instance, was for Erskine "not *a mere act* on account of which God blesses [us], but it was and is a living principle reproducing itself in the hearts and lives of those who receive it" (Election, p. 373). Or, one can see the same concept in the opening paragraphs of *The Brazen Serpent*. Erskine begins with a narration of the story of Nicodemus (in John 3:1-14) but then moves swiftly to a delineation of the "principles' inherent in the story, the chief of which is the eternal principle of new life, or of the life-giving power of the Gospel (which in fact is the central theme elucidated at great length throughout the book). It is here, the, that we can see why Erskine was at no time committed to a narrow biblical literalism: that an event recorded in the Bible might not have been an actual event or that the record itself was not historically accurate, such matters were not of immediate concern to him.

Because he was primarily interested in communicating the principle(s) inherent in a given biblical passage, Erskine could sometimes treat the text of Scripture in a seemingly off-hand manner, almost playfully at times. He was wont on occasion to revise the *textus receptus*, to emend it, or even correct it. One "lighthearted" example is his rendering of Psalm 42:1: "Even as the heart panteth after the water-brooks, so would my soul pant after that fountain of life, and light, and joy." Erskine's interpretative imagination can be seen, again, in his unabashed identification of the "ladder" in Jacob's dream (Gen. 28:11-17) with Jesus Christ:

On him [Christ]...the soul can mount to God, and to the place where God dwells, surrounded by the love and praise of blessed angels and redeemed sinners, and down the ladder the blessings of God, the gifts of the Spirit, and the intimations of his loving-kindness descend to us. (Hanna, p. 84)

Erskine also discerned the presence of Jesus in the Psalms, either as subject or as actual speaker. In Psalm 40:9 ("I have preached righteousness in the great congregation.") the voice is "certainly none other than the Savior" (Election, p. 216). And in Psalm 130:1 ("Out of the depths have I cried unto thee, O Lord."), he who cries out of his human nature is "no other than our Lord Jesus Christ" (Serpent, 21, 121). Apart from specific verses in the Psalter, Erskine said that "we find Jesus" throughout the Psalms "continually confessing as one of the sinful race on whom the Lord had laid the iniquity of all" (Election, p. 235).[10]

Not only did Erskine interpret biblical texts in this often fanciful manner, he also could allude to or cite chapter and verse pedagogically, so as both to illustrate a point he was making and to inform or "teach" his correspondent. "Be sure to read John 17," or "Remember what Paul wrote in Romans 11," or "What you say makes me think of the parable of the prodigal"--such statements, allusions, and suggestions, since they appear so frequently, cannot but reflect Erskine's having been totally immersed in Scripture. There is the charming anecdote told of the time when, in 1847, Erskine cause to have constructed a well on the Arbroath road just north of the Fintry Bridge; the well was Erskine's gift to the townsfolk, and on it he had the builders place the inscription (from John 4:14) "Whoever drinks of this water shall thirst again."[11]

If Erskine could, as it were, play with biblical texts, interpret them at times in his own peculiar manner, or employ them with a kind of didactic intent, he could also take the problems associated with biblical translations with utmost seriousness. Not only did he feel called upon at times to emend the Greek text of the New Testament (Sp. Order, pp. 180f), but more often he felt constrained to point out errors in the Authorized Version (which he called the "common English version"). There are passages, he said, which throw "no light, but rather darkness, on the character of God," and other passages which are 'as incorrect as [they are] uninstructive" (Election, pp. 124f). Or again: "Our translators have lost to the English reader the entire instruction intended...to be conveyed" (Election, p. 120). Erskine insisted, for instance, that the word "impute," which appears several times in Romans 4, was both a theologically and linguistically misleading translation since it implied a "fictitious transaction" between God and humankind. Would not, he suggested, words such as "reckon" or "consider" or "account" be more faithful translations of the original? (Election, p. 244)[12] Similarly, he was convinced that it would be more accurate to render "the grace of God...hath abounded unto many" (Rom. 5:15) as "abounded unto *all*." Clearly Erskine's own theological views (in

CHAPTER FIVE: BIBLICAL AUTHORITY 65

this last case, his universalism)led him to make such suggestions. Clearly, too, when he accused the Calvinists of eisegesis (of reading "double predestination," for instance, *into* the text of Romans 9), it was an accusation of which Erskine was himself not wholly innocent. Erskine did say, however (perhaps aware of his own temptation to make a text coincide with his own theological sensitivities), that the translator's responsibility, since errors have surely crept into the received text, was to aim, not so much at a literal rendering as to express the 'true sense" of the passage under consideration. (Here again, as with Erskine's emphasis on "principles," one sees why Erskine could never have been a biblical literalist.) Accordingly, when undertaking the exposition of some scriptural text, Erskine would often make his own translation. One illuminating example is his rendering of Romans 5:17:

> And thus if by the offence of one, death hath reigned through that one, that is, by the participation of his nature, much more shall those who accept the grace and gift of righteousness which abound unto all, reign in life through the other man, Jesus Christ, that is, by the participation of his nature.

> (The A.V. reads: For if by one man's offence death reigned by one; much more they which receive abundance of grace and of the gift of righteousness shall reign in life by one, Jesus Christ.)

Erskine did have the grace to admit that his translation was in fact more of a "paraphrase" than a word-for-word translation, yet at the same time he felt strongly that his version was more faithful to the "sense" of the original. In another place Erskine asked his readers not to "condemn" a free translation of his (in this case, of Romans 8:26-30), but to examine it so as to discern whether or not it was more faithful to the original (i.e., Greek) than the "common translation" (Election, p. 394).

Since Erskine had so strong a proclivity for omitting words from the text, for changing words or adding words, and for making his own "free translations" or "paraphrases," one might not inappropriately ask whether his frequent assertions as to the truth and authority of Scripture were genuine. Yet, given Erskine's kaleidoscopic approach to Scripture, that may be the wrong question to ask in as much as it is not patient of a simple "yes" or "no" answer. What an anonymous reviewer (of the second volume of Hanna's *Letters of Thomas Erskine*) wrote may be helpful in respect to such a question:

> [Erskine] was roused to almost passionate utterance because he saw all round him how the Scriptures, instead of being regarded as sent to us to brighten and nourish the light within, had become a bushel under which the light was hidden. It was to him a self-evident

proposition that *mere authority* is valid for all creeds alike, and consequently for none, and that the sure way to dishonour the Bible was *not* to submit its statements to the judgment [of] conscience.[13]

This comment suggests — rightly, I believe — that Scripture was indeed authoritative for Erskine but that its authority was neither objective nor exterior to the reader; rather, biblical authority was interior. As Erskine himself wrote: "The Bible tells us of things which are true in our own hearts, it does not make them true" (Election, p. 67). Or, even more forcefully:

> Whatever truth there may be in any [biblical] doctrine, it is not true to me...until I find it witnessed to, and sealed by a sense of light and truth in my own heart--it must be translated into a language which my heart understands--it must meet and tally with a living consciousness within me, else it is of no use to me. (Election, pp. 219f)

In these passages, Erskine's use of the word "heart" is typical but not always exact. More often than not, "heart" is synonymous with "conscience": God is in one's conscience, God addresses the conscience, God illumines the conscience. Conscience is, in fact, the "meeting place" between us and God. It is therefore within the conscience ("heart") that resides the norm by which one assesses or tests the authority and meaning of Scripture. Yet Erskine is not always exact in his terminology, as seen in his statement that "[i]n the Bible, the heart generally means the whole mind and does not stand for the affections exclusively, as it does in our common language" (Faith, p. 40). These apparent discrepancies notwithstanding, Erskine did quite consistently point to the conscience as the human arbiter and receptor of divine truth, whether biblical truth or not. In a metaphor that is not without its difficulties, Erskine wrote that the "conscience is the eye" and "the Bible is the telescope; and as the telescope does not change the faculty of sight, but brings more objects within its range, so does the Bible to the conscience" (Hanna, p. 218). Or, more simply: "I feel that I believe the Bible because of the things I find in it, rather than that I believe them because they are in the Bible" (Hanna, pp. 410f).

In a recently published article on Erskine's understanding of authority, Steve Gowler has emphasized this point:

> According to Erskine, the customary view [of biblical inspiration] has its argument precisely backwards when it maintains that the Bible is true and trustworthy because it is inspired. Rather, it can be justifiably called inspired because what it tells us about God and ourselves is discovered to be true in the context of our moral experience.[14]

CHAPTER FIVE: BIBLICAL AUTHORITY 67

Erskine's perception of biblical authority as we have seen was first articulated in a sustained manner is his 1820 publication, *Remarks on the Internal Evidence for the Truth of Revealed Religion*. Yet the seeds of his later thinking were, by his own testimony, already in his consciousness from an early date. As he wrote to Shairp (in 1863): "One of my earliest convictions, when I first apprehended the meaning of Christianity, was that, however much we might learn truth from the Bible, as soon as we had learned it, we found that we held it on a much deeper and more unshakable ground than the authority of the bible, namely, on its own discerned truthfulness."[15] It is no surprise, therefore, that Erskine became increasingly critical of those who looked to the Bible as an "infallible book." In making such criticisms, he insisted that he was not detracting from or minimizing the authority of the Bible, he was merely putting it in its proper place. Julia Wedgwood recorded a conversation she had with Erskine in which she asked him, "Do we not want now to be delivered from an infallible book, as in the time of Luther from an infallible Church?" Erskine was quick to agree and replied that the two were "the same kind of evil" (Hanna, p. 366). Indeed, he was convinced that to rely on the objective inerrancy of Scripture was to fall into submissive fideism, to abrogate one's obligation of apprehending the truth in the light of one's conscience, and to substitute implicit obedience for a lively and living faith (Election, p. 515).[16] Erskine wrote in a similar vein to Archibald Campbell Tait: "The bible is given me to help me to know God...and if I take a belief in the Bible as a substitute for that loving trust in God, I am a great loser...An infallible book would be as injurious to our real spiritual education as an infallible man. It would allow us to rest satisfied short of God" (Ewing, IV.55f).[17]

If, for Erskine, the authority of Scripture was not an objective, exterior authority, and if the Bible was therefore not to be treated as an infallible book before which the reader was to sit in passive, submissive obedience, it is surely consistent with such views that Erskine would, on several occasions, give voice to his ultimate independence from Scripture. In what at first glance appears at best to be an oxymoron and at worst an exercise in futile logic, Erskine wrote to Alexander Ewing, "Only as the bible commends itself to my conscience will I acknowledge its authority — then I will no longer need to acknowledge its authority" (Ewing, IV.58).[18] It appears that Erskine could make such a statement because, for all his being a "man of the Bible," the Bible for him was not an object of faith. Knowledge of the Bible, then, however extensive, cannot replace or be a substitute of one's perception and experience of God. Further, a faith in God that finds security in the infallibility or verbal inspiration of the Bible is no real faith; at least, it is no faith *in God*. This conviction led Erskine to claim that, even if the Bible is where God and the conscience meet, God is surely not limited to the medium of the Bible alone to effect such meeting. This means, of course, that Erskine abandoned his earlier view of the Bible as the *only* source for divine knowledge or Christian doctrine. Even "a man without the Bible," he said, "has still a God, and a God whom he can get acquainted with through his conscience" (Hanna, p. 218). Or, again: "We may know the Bible and not God, [and] we may know God and not the Bible" (Hanna, p. 365). Even more pointedly: "When it is not God Himself we meet and trust in His word, we are breaking the second commandment" (Hanna, p. 192). It was even possible, thought Erskine, to be "entirely unacquainted with Jewish or Christian Scriptures" and yet to have a filial relation of trust with God, to discern God's purpose for one's life, to possess true faith, to be "in Christ," and to know what it means to be created in God's image (Hanna, p. 433). Surely some of Erskine's friends must have been, if not scandalized, at least alarmed by Erskine's assertion that God can be communicated "even to those whom no Bible or no missionary has ever reached" (Election, p. 156).

It is in such sentiments that we see Erskine's underlying concept of biblical authority. On a relatively superficial level he seemed convinced, at least as testified to in his early writings, that the Bible was the one and only sure authority ("The Spirit never acts except through the medium of the doctrines of the Bible."); later he believed that God could indeed address one's conscience apart from, or through some other medium than, the Bible. And, on one occasion, at least, he anticipated Coleridge and Benjamin Jowett by suggesting that, if there is no ultimate distinction between sacred and secular, then we should read the Bible as we do any other book: "When I read Plato or Shakespeare in a spirit entirely different from that in which I allow myself to read the Bible, I am wrong" (Hanna, pp. 383f).[19] In Shakespeare's *Macbeth*, for instance, he could discern "the terrible judgment of conscience upon sin," and in Plato's *Gorgias* a clear adumbration of the Christian doctrines of atonement and justification by faith.[20] In a word, if one could meet God in the Bible, it would be an error to suppose or claim that God was limited to the Bible or that the Bible was the sole medium for such encounters. If "the Bible was given to us, not to be cited as a peremptory authority in anything, but to help us understand the "character of God" (Hanna, p. 429), then, Erskine believed, the experience of, or potential for, one's encounter with God belonged to the whole of one's life and to the whole context of one's life. As important as the Bible was to the effecting of such encounters, God's dealings with humankind could not be restricted to claims of biblical infallibility; such claims, we have seen, would be nothing short of idolatry.

In spite of Erskine's comparatively liberal views in respect to the authority of Scripture, the rise of biblical criticism presented him with many problems. These problems, however, did not stem from his feeling that such criticism either challenged or impugned the truths to be discerned in Scripture. He may indeed have experienced "anxiety and not a little alarm" (Hanna, p. 575) with the publication of *Essays and Reviews* (1860), Renan's *La Vie de Jésus* (1863), Seeley's *Ecce Homo* (1865), and Colenso's *The Pentateuch and the Book of Joshua Critically Examined* (1862-79), but his anxiety was quite clearly a "pastoral" one. Biblical criticism *per se* did not worry him; his concern, rather, was with the effect such criticism might

CHAPTER FIVE: BIBLICAL AUTHORITY

have on those for whom inerrant verbal inspiration or exclusive biblical authority were the bed-rock of their faith. The Bible, he said, was a book for "beginners" as well as for the initiated, and it was these beginners, therefore, that might be swept away in the current of biblical criticism. Of Colenso's work Erskine wrote (to John McLeod Campbell) that it seemed to "sap the foundation of traditional faith" (Hanna, p. 433), and to Ewing he wrote: "I must make my protest against the principle that Theology is nothing more than Biblical criticism, or interpretation of texts and words" (Ewing, IV.40). If the events recorded in the Book of Exodus were shown to be historically inaccurate, such a discovery could very well "shake much of that faith which does not rest on God alone" (Hanna, p. 433), and to the Bishop of Natal himself he wrote a long (undated) letter in which the following observations are to be found:

> If all the religious teachers of this country, or even a large proportion of them, did really in their teaching address the conscience and reason of their people, so that the people were accustomed to this kind of [critical] thought, I do not believe that your books could have excited any alarm; but you know well that this is not the case, and that conventional notions on religion are the common notions of the country, and that, generally speaking, Christianity itself is identified with, and is supposed to stand on nothing else than, the belief of the verbal inspiration of the Bible. This wrong state of things ought certainly to be corrected as speedily as possible. But by what means? It is a difficult question...(Hanna, p. 399).

Because of his liberal views in respect to biblical authority, Erskine was not himself troubled by the rise of biblical criticism; at the same time he feared for those whose conservative views saw in such criticism a genuine danger. Yet, for Erskine, that conservative faith was shallow, something to be "corrected as speedily as possible." He spoke, for instance, of his own land of Scotland where "a belief in the Bible is often substituted for a faith in God," and where the discovery of any contradiction or inaccuracy in the gospel history would lead to a person's "whole faith" being "annihilated." But such faith, he added, was a faith that rested on ignorance; it was "not the kind of faith which we would desire for ourselves or others" (Hanna, p. 400).

There is certainly a degree of irony here, if not some overt ambivalence on Erskine's part. On the one hand, Erskine was not troubled by biblical criticism because he believed the truth of Scripture transcended the text of the Bible itself. On the other hand, he expressed concerns for those whose faith might be endangered by such criticisms. Yet if this concern on Erskine's part was genuine (and I believe it was), it was also condescending. The writings of a Colenso or a Jowett, he felt, might have--indeed, would have--serious consequences for those "beginners" in

Scotland and elsewhere who held to a "traditional faith," whose faith did not "rest on God alone," who subscribed to "conventional" or "common" notions, or whose faith in the Bible was a "substitute" for faith in God.[21] It appears that Erskine was giving voice here to a double standard, one which separated the beginners from the initiates. Biblical criticism was an unwanted threat to the former and a matter of little consequence to the latter. Yet there are some indications that Erskine did not stand dispassionately above the storm created by biblical criticism. If he gave evidence of "devotion to the Bible and [at the same time a] rejection of verbal inspiration,"[22] it may be that he was less troubled by the biblical critics' conclusions than by disregard for the implications such conclusions would certainly have for the majority of Christian folk: "It was their rationalistic tone and the impression it created in the public mind [that] repelled [Erskine]."[23] And the irony of all this is pointed out in Olive Brose's suggestion that the "crises" presented by biblical criticism "never presented a problem for [Erskine]," and the deeper reason for this was that his "world was not that of the rationalist, critical-scientific nineteenth century, but quite completely that of the Bible."[24]

Erskine's understanding of and approach to biblical authority was at best a complicated matter. He balanced (precariously) a deep commitment to the truth contained exclusively in Scripture with an avowed independence from Scripture; too, he balanced (ambivalently) a disregard (on the part of the "initiates") for the consequences of biblical criticisms with a pastoral concern for the effect such consequences might have on the "beginners." Or, to put it another way, he was at pains to point out the need to correct the prevailing attitude towards biblical inspiration (but "By what means?") while at the same time asking "Is there any valid and unshakable protection against the fears...stirred up" by critical inquiries in Scripture? (Sp. Order, p. 77)

Yet cutting across these seemingly disjointed, if not contradictory, attitudes on Erskine's part was his conviction that neither the Bible nor the critics of the Bible were infallible; ultimate authority for divine truth rested in neither. Therefore, to those whose faith was threatened as well as to those whose faith was no longer based on submissive obedience to exterior authority (biblical or critical), he could say: "There is no true religion except the love of God abiding in the heart...[Therefore], however much we know the Bible, we have only as much knowledge of God as we have love, and no more" (Sp. Order, pp. 132, 135). Surely Erskine both knew his Bible and loved his God. And his high hope was that men and women would seek more to love God than to boast in their knowledge of the Bible, since, for him, God was not only the one whose character was revealed in Scripture, God was also a loving God who invites us into his household even as we invite him into our hearts. Therein lies the truth and the authority of the Christian religion. So it was not mere idiosyncratic playfulness that led Erskine on occasion to alter the text of Scripture, since there were for him truths deeper than

CHAPTER FIVE: BIBLICAL AUTHORITY

the words of Scripture itself. For this reason, then, he could say with remarkable confidence and assurance: "Even as the heart panteth after the water-brooks, so would my soul pant after that fountain of life, and light, and joy."

Notes to Chapter Five

[1] *Confessio Fidei Westmonasteriensis*, I.1.

[2] *Acts of the General Assembly of the Church of Scotland, 1638-1842* (Edinburgh, 1843), p. 158; cited by A.C. Cheyne, *The Transforming of the Kirk* (Edinburgh: Saint Andrew Press, 1983), p. 10. "The chief difficulty [for Christianity in Scotland]," wrote Erskine to Alexander Ewing, "Consists in the existing Confession of Faith and Articles to which the clergy feel themselves bound. This is a great evil; but we can scarcely look for any deliverance from it, because the clerical body could never agree among themselves as to the changes which should be made on the symbols" (Ewing, IV.29).

[3] Robert A. Reid, *The Influence, Indirect and Indirect, of the Writings of Erskine of Linlathen on Religious Thought in Scotland* (Thesis, New College, Edinburgh, 1930), p. 53. This work, albeit containing some valuable insights, is more of an "appreciation" of Erskine than a critical study of his theology. It may have been an unwitting testimony to the nature of this appreciation that led Reid to refer mistakenly (p. 253) to Erskine's *Internal Evidence* as *Eternal Evidence*!

[4] Erskine wrote to his cousin Rachel that the exquisite hymns in Keble's *the Christian Year* are "worth more, in my mind, [than] the whole shorter and Longer Catechisms together" (Hanna, p. 112).

[5] A similar sentiment was voiced by George Eliot: "So long as a belief in propositions is regarded as indispensable to salvation, the pursuit of truth as such is not possible." "Evangelical Teaching: Dr. Cumming," *Westminster Review* (Oct., 1855).

[6] A further example of the controversial rhetoric that swirled around Erskine is Andrew Thomson's rather startling statement, in his review of Robert Burns' *the Gairloch Heresy Tried*, that we "would express our gratitude to the author for having taken up the subject [of Erskine], and for having treated it in so popular and useful a manner. 'Small shot,' he himself observes, 'it may be termed,' but what of that; it does the necessary execution. A rifle may strike down an opponent as effectively as the heaviest piece of ordnance." *Edinburgh Christian Instructor*, 29 (Feb., 1830), pp. 117f.

[7] This, the reader will notice, is not an accurate quotation on Erskine's part.

[8] To Colenso Erskine wrote: "The value of the Bible...consists in what it contains,--in the truth which I find in it,--not in the manner in which it was composed" (Hanna, p. 398).

[9] Julia Wedgwood has made the same observation: "Whether an event actually took place or not was less important [to Erskine] than whether or not it illustrated any great principle." "Thomas Erskine of Linlathen," in *Nineteenth Century Teachers and Other Essays* (London: Hodder & Stoughton, 1909), p. 68.

[10] Cf. Isaiah 53:6. Christ is also the "speaker" in Ps. 18:23 and the "subject of Ps. 74:3! Interestingly, Erskine posits Moses as the author of the 90th Psalm. An example of Erskine's custom of inserting biblical allusions into his letters can be seen in a short note he wrote to John McLeod Campbell: "I have been reading over the 12th, 13th, and 14th of First Corinthians. It is a very remarkable passage. Paul seems to have been almost as troubled by

these manifestations as Irving was, and he seems to have escaped by seeing that they did not stand in the authoritative place that Irving assigned them. The 19th verse of the 14th chapter gives me the same impression that I used to receive from a comparison of the Row teaching with the Port-Glasgow manifestations thirty-two years ago" (Hanna, p. 341).

11 J. Malcolm, *The Parish of Monifieth in Ancient and Modern Times* (London: Wm. Green & Sons, 1910), pp. 278f.

12 A further discussion of "imputation" as a "fiction of law" is found in Election, pp. 327-334.

13 Anon., Review of Hanna, *The Letters of Thomas Erskine*, Vol. 2, *The Spectator* (Dec. 29, 1877), p. 1662.

14 Steve Gowler, "No Second-Hand Religion," *Church History*, 54 (June, 1985), p. 209. Alexander Ewing tells the delightful story of a young man from India who, after reading Erskine's *Freeness*, remarked: "If I could believe in supernatural inspiration at all, it would be in that of Mr. Erskine of Linlathen" (Ewing, IV.75).

15 Quoted by W.A. Knight, *Principal Shairp and His Friends* (London: John Murray, 1888) p. 211.

16 "[T]o reduce all belief into submissive obedience," wrote Erskine elsewhere, "is as a great a blunder in religion as it is in common sense. I cannot become loving or pure or humble by mere obedience" (Hanna, p. 398).

17 Earlier Erskine had made a similar remark: "We are not called upon to believe the Bible merely that we may give proof of our willingness to submit in all things to God's authority, but that we may be influenced by the object of our belief" (Faith, p. 25).

18 Julia Wedgwood quotes Erskine as having said the same thing to her: "I think we shall learn to value the Bible more as we grow independent of it" (Hanna, p. 355).

19 This statement, in a letter to Mrs. Burnett, is dated 17 March 1840, the same year in which Coleridge's *Confessions of an Inquiring Spirit* was posthumously published and two decades prior to the appearance, in *Essays and Reviews*, and of Benjamin Jowett's "On the Interpretation of Scripture."

20 Hanna, pp. 182, 434, and 460. Erskine also said that he could not draw a distinction between inspiration "in the bible" and inspiration "out of the Bible," since he was sure that God could speak to us directly in the "secret of our own being." He nevertheless admitted that what he found in the Old and New Testament reached his soul "with a conviction and power that I find in no other thoughts and words" (Hanna, p. 402).

21 Erskine was hardly the only person to claim that the rise of biblical criticism was sure to be injurious to the faith of many Christians. See, for instance, the references in Josef L. Altholz, "The Mind of Victorian Orthodoxy: Anglican Responses to 'Essays and Reviews,' 1860-1864," *Church History*, 51 (1982), pp. 186-197.

22 Gowler, *op. cit.*, p. 210.

23 A.L. Drummond and J. Bulloch, *The Church in Victorian Scotland* (Edinburgh: Saint Andrew Press, 1975), p. 254.

24 Olive Brose, *Frederick Denison Maurice* (Athens: Ohio University Press, 1971), pp. 44f.

CHAPTER SIX: THE CHARACTER OF GOD

> I am unable to conceive how I have the consciousness of a separate existence from my Creator ... I have never been a single moment separated from Him. It is impossible that I should be separated from Him without ceasing to exist. (Freeness, pp. 23, 25)

In June of 1826 Erskine wrote to his friend Merle D'Aubigné, "Oh, what I wish for is that spiritual eye, and ear, and heart that might see, and hear, and feel God in everything" (Hanna, p. 55). It might be said that Erskine's subsequent career as author and lay theologian was committed to the fulfillment of that passionate desire to see, hear, and feel God — a desire that must surely have been born out of the longed for experience itself. His was a commitment, too, to the hope that he might assist others to pursue the same goal and to discover in God a loving and intimate friend. Yet many difficulties in respect to so ambitious a vocation presented themselves to Erskine. Parallel to his query, for instance, as to how the pervasive belief in the verbal inspiration of the Bible might be "corrected as speedily as possible," was his concern as to how one might present a belief in a living and loving God to a generation brought up under the deadening influences of a stern Calvinism. If, as Erskine had written, it was possible to know the Bible and not God, it was equally possible to use one's religion as a cloak to hide or disguise one's lack of belief. As Erskine had, in his earlier writings, inveighed against the superstition and idolatry that marked the "religion of the land," so too he continued to believe that

> where the living personality of God is lost, there is atheism. And this is the case now ... [T]he name of God and the forms of morality are retained, and therefore the age thinks itself a religious and God-fearing age, but it is not the *living God* that is worshipped. Men have a *religion* instead of a *God*. This is their atheism, this is their shield against God. (Serpent, p. 226)

In addition to this covert "atheism" that Erskine discerned around him, there was in much of contemporary religion a tendency, he thought, toward vapid theological abstraction. A cold, rational, metaphysical labyrinth which talked endlessly about God was more in evidence than a vibrant, fertile faith in, and apprehension of, God. The former produces but a "vague affection" for an "ill-defined" object, while only the latter can make a lasting impress on the human spirit.[1] "Many have much information about God," wrote Erskine, "who have never yet thought of listening to his voice, to and in themselves" (Election, p. 90). Such persons are given to proclaiming "notions," however sophisticated, while what we need is a faith that leads us, "personally and consciously," to meet God in our own hearts (Election, pp. 226f).[2] Without a sense of God's nearness, or without an awareness of the living reality that is God, religion becomes a mere set of notions — and "a great deal of the Christianity of our day is of this spurious kind." But, when the indwelling presence of God animates and fills our Christian doctrines, then it is that these "mere notions will melt into nothing" (Freeness, pp. 19f). Erskine's abiding impatience, throughout his life, was with that brand of theologizing which led people to treat the "name" of God as a plaything to be bandied about in religious discourse or debate, a "name" to be speculated upon or argued over. This was not to *know* God, as Erskine was to say time and again, since God can be known only by the "desire of the heart" (Freeness, p. 132).

For all his dissatisfaction with, and criticisms of, the contemporary theological enterprise, Erskine was also aware of his own shortcomings in this respect. If he could criticize others, he could criticize himself as well. He wrote, for instance, to Bishop Ewing that "[i]t may be that we have both of us been occupied in excogitating answers to unanswerable difficulties rather than acquainting ourselves with God himself. I have heard God say that to *me,* and I have felt the truth and the voice of reproof, and desire to profit by it" (Ewing, I.46).[3] Such a confession on Erskine's part indicates, perhaps, that he was aware that theological doctrines, dogmas, or systematic constructs cannot, in and of themselves, capture the truth or exhaust the meaning they intend to convey; they are but symbols or signposts pointing, one hopes, toward God as the object of belief and cannot therefore themselves be objects of belief. Not being in the least a "systematic" theologian — being in fact somewhat suspicious of "systems" — Erskine was not given to expound on the major theological tenets of classical orthodoxy (and, it must be said, he was neither fully familiar with nor sympathetic with classical orthodoxy). The doctrine of the Trinity is a case in point: at no time did he attempt to discuss or interpret so prominent a doctrine of the Christian tradition; in fact, he dismissed it in a word or two.[4] And, not surprisingly, he dismissed the doctrine of "transubstantiation" out of hand. Referring to the controversies which were distressing the Church of England in response to the publication of *Essays and Reviews*, Erskine wrote to Dean Stanley:

> In this whole discussion there seems to me to lurk the idea that the dogmas of Christianity are imposed on us not as helps or guides, but as exercises of obedience and submission. I believe, on the contrary, that they are given for the purpose of explaining to us our relations with the spiritual world. (Hanna, p. 345)

And, in a subsequent letter to Stanley's wife, Lady Augusta, Erskine elaborated further on this theme:

> There is a point which I have often wished to see more illustrated and enforced than it is generally, and that is the adoption of Christian dogma (when believed) to produce the Christian character.

CHAPTER SIX: THE CHARACTER OF GOD

Paul speaks of the Gospel as being THE POWER *of God unto salvation*, that is, as containing the *dynamics*, so to speak, the spiritual lever, and ropes, and pulleys, and wheel by which the human spirit may be lifted out of the horrible pit and miry clay of sin and selfishness into a harmony with the mind of God, so that a real apprehension of the character of God and His purposes towards us, and our relation to Him, without any mention of the precepts, would spontaneously produce the life of them within our souls. (Hanna, p. 347)

It is quite apparent that Erskine approached formal articulations of Christian doctrine in much the same way as he approached Scripture. Neither passive submission to an external authority (scriptural or doctrinal or ecclesiastic), nor a turning of religion into a catena of abstract notions would do. *Theology*, for him, was precisely what the word means: "discourse with God" (or, it may be that he would have preferred "conversation" with God). Accordingly, both Bible and doctrine, when understood in relation to their purpose, could be — and should be — the context or locus within which the character of God makes an indelible impress on the human character. For Erskine, God was both the subject and the object of theological endeavor, or, more accurately, the relation between God and humankind was at the very heart of genuine theology: Who God is for us and who we are for God.[5] Christian doctrine, as distinct from precept, means simply the "discovery of the relation in which God stands to man" (Sp. Order, p. 259).

Erskine described this relation as having two aspects: it indicates our distance from God as well as our closeness to God. There is, that is, within the human condition an "alienation" which God is constantly seeking to overcome. And it can be best overcome, paradoxically, by God's intimate closeness to us, by God's abiding fellowship with us. Graphically, it is as if distance and closeness were two foci which hold the theological ellipse in tension. Each focus is true of the divine/human relation. But when one of the foci — alienation — is removed, the ellipse reverts immediately into a circle, at the very center of which we and God mutually indwell each other. This mutual indwelling — a relation of untold intimacy — is both a future hope and, proleptically, a present reality. "Who God is for us," and "who we are for God," might more appropriately be stated as "Who is God in us," and "who we are in God." I have previously pointed out that one of the biblical texts to which Erskine often referred is 2 Peter 1:4 ("Whereby are given to us exceeding great and precious promises: that by these ye might be partakers of the divine nature."). And with equal frequency, throughout the whole course of his writings, he made similar or related assertions. "The object [of God's love] is that we should be made partakers of the life of God" (Serpent, p. 93). Again: "Did God indeed grudge our being as gods? Nay, he has suffered ... that we might be partakers of the divine nature" (*ibid.*, p. 269, n. 1). Yet again: "Eternity is to my mind just the same thing as God, and when I lose myself in eternity, I feel that I lose myself in God" (Hanna, p. 57). It is one's "love of God" that produces in the believer a "likeness to God" (Faith, p. 47). Similarly, it is by loving God that we come to "resemble God" (Rutherford, p. xxv). "The whole use of the gospel," wrote Erskine, "is to introduce the holy love of God into man's heart, that it may work there its own likeness" (Freeness, p. 91).

This mutual indwelling of God and this concept of mutual participation was for Erskine a reality born out of experience. He could no more deny it, he said, than, were he in a darkened room when a candle was lit, he could fail to notice the light (Serpent, p. 8).

To speak so personally and intimately about one's relation to God was a rare phenomenon in Erskine's day. It is not surprisingly, therefore, that some of Erskine's adversaries complained of his religious pretensions, believing that he spoke too familiarly and too presumptuously of God, claiming for himself a privileged relationship to the Deity. The formidable Andrew Thomson, for instance, was keenly disturbed by Erskine's language of mutual participation (albeit such language clearly has biblical precedents!). With characteristic vigor he complained that Erskine "is in danger of believing himself an emanation of the Supreme Being — of mixing himself with the Divine essence — of mistaking himself for a portion of the Divinity."[6] Archibald Robertson was no less exercised. "Our limited capacities can comprehend only a small part of the doings of God," he wrote, going on to give the explicit impression that Erskine aspired to divine knowledge that was beyond the reach of human knowing.[7] Erskine never responded to such gratuitous accusations, but had he, he might very well have said that, for him, it was more important to know who God was than to worry about who Thomas Erskine was![8]

Unquestionably the abiding attribute of God to which Erskine sought diligently to witness was that of love, a love so intense and so inextinguishable that it was as if God loved the individual person so passionately that it seemed as if there were no other individuals to love. This love, however, was not a romantic or sentimental attribute. Rather, it was a love that went out to "meet the natural cry of misery and the weary and undefined cravings of the unsatisfied spirit" (Faith, p. 45). Erskine believed that for too many people God was the "enemy," a Deity whose a punitive judgment was to be feared, a Sovereign whose wrath was at all costs to be avoided or propitiated (Baxter, p. xxv). A truer and more accurate image, thought Erskine, was that of a God who was to the human spirit what a keystone is to an arch — remove it, and the arch crumbles (Freeness, p. 6). Even so, we can trust that, however often we crumble because we do not experience God's supportive presence, God will restore the keystone, himself. Access to God and to God's love is constantly available, and God yearns for people to avail themselves of so rich a gift. God invites all people to "come in"; God's inviting arms are "always open" (Freeness, pp. 8, 86). The Fall in no way destroyed or annihilated God's love for us; it only impaired our vision as to the limitless extent of God's love. God, wrote Erskine, is like a "Father" who will never abandon his children; God is like a "Mother" who will never forget those she has suckled; nor will she forget the children of her womb: "Yea, they may forget, yet I will not forget thee" (Hanna, p. 426).[9]

God's love, wrote Erskine, is not to be construed as "omnipotence" (although he does often describe it as "powerful"); it is not a coercive or demanding or overpowering love. Nor is it a love offered only to those who are "pure in heart." God loves *every* person, even in the loathsomeness of their pollution, even in their posture of bitterest enmity, even in their arrogant atheism. God loves so universally and so extravagantly that he was willing to taste death for us all (Serpent, p. 68). This emphasis on the sacrificial nature of God's love appears in Erskine's writings as early as 1822, although at first somewhat problematically:

> The exhibition of the Divine character ... must not only be consistent with its own excellence, but also suited to make an impression on the reason and the feelings of the guilty. And it is so. The Judge himself bore the punishment of transgression, while he published an amnesty to the guilty, and thus asserted the authority and importance of the law, by that very act which beamed forth love unspeakable, and displayed a compassion which knew no obstacle but the unwillingness of the criminals to accept it. The Eternal Word became flesh; and exhibited in sufferings and in death that combination of holiness and mercy which, if believed, must excite love, and if loved, must produce resemblance ... A pardon without sacrifice could have made but a weak and obscure appeal. (Evidence, p. 49)

Or, as Erskine was to write later, in a little essay entitled "On Love," appended to his *The Brazen Serpent*:

> Love is the name of God ... [I]t is a grieved and grieving love, it is the very love which wept and groaned and agonised in Jesus. The sufferings of Jesus were not a manifestation of a passing temporary thing; they were the manifestation of the mind of the unchangeable God towards sinful man. (Serpent, pp. 286ff)

It cannot be argued, therefore, as many of Erskine's detractors did argue, that his views as to the universality of God's suffering love were ultimately either a theological absurdity on his part or else a flagrant example of "heretical" antinomianism. The principle of sacrifice so consistently advocated by Erskine is clear evidence to the contrary.[10]

For Erskine, then, God's love is characterized by mutual indwelling, by universality, and by sacrifice. It is also a *patient* love. Perhaps the most frequently quoted passage from all of Erskine's writing is this:

> He who waited so long for the formation of a piece of old red sandstone will surely wait with much long-suffering for the perfection of a human spirit. (Hanna, p. 427)[11]

"God," in fact, "is in no hurry" (*Ibid.*, p. 351). Or, again: "There is no haste with God" (Sp. Order, p. 52). And a clear indication that Erskine believed that the "perfecting of a human spirit" is not limited to an individual's life-time, but can be effected even beyond the barrier of death, can be seen in his subsequent revision of the earlier quotation (this time in response to a question he poses to himself — What are the prospects for those outside the Christian pale, ... for those given to profligacy and vice, or for those addicted to sensual gratification or selfish pursuits?):

> He who has taken untold ages for the formation of a bit of old red sandstone may not be limited to three score years and ten for the perfecting of a human spirit. (Sp. Order, p. 53)

It would be, not only unreasonable, but actually "monstrous," thought Erskine, to suppose that God's purposes for us could be thwarted once we quit this world, even if we had spent all our days resisting God's efforts to bring us out of death into life. So to limit God would be to dishonor him who said, "I will never leave thee, nor forsake thee," or "The mountains shall depart, and the hills be removed, but my kindness shall not depart from thee, neither shall the covenant of my peace be removed" (Hanna, pp. 423f and Ewing IV.66).[12]

God's love is not an "elective" love, choosing some but not others. And, as a love offered to all, it is quite specifically a *purposeful* love. And since the purpose of God lies eternally in the Divine heart, it can in no way be set aside or withdrawn. Erskine describes this in a variety of ways. God's intention is that the character of human beings is to be brought into harmony with, and reflect, the divine character. God strives to meet the weary and undefined cravings of the unsatisfied human spirit. "God sees us as we are, yet with a love that always desires to make us what we should be — like Himself; and which will eternally persist in urging the accomplishment of that desire" (Sp. Order, p. 242). God's love yearns painfully for a response of love. Our sin will in no way divert God from being our God nor cause God to abandon us. God, in a word, will not give up. Erskine articulates this with consistent force: "God's purpose of unchanging love ... will never cease its striving till it has engaged every child of man ... In coming to this conclusion, it is manifest that I am constrained to adopt the assurance that this purpose follows man out from his present life, through all stages of being that lie before him; unto its full accomplishment" (Sp. Order, p. 69). Or, as he wrote succinctly nearly a half century earlier, "Death remains, but there is promise of new and endless life beyond the grave" (Freeness, p. 8).

Erskine was not a few times accused of not taking sin seriously; concomitantly, he was also accused of not taking God's holiness and righteousness seriously. "[M]en are entreated, beseeched, and urged," an anonymous critic wrote, "by the mercies *and the terrors* of the Lord, to believe in the Lord Jesus Christ ..."[13] Nothing could be further from Erskine's understanding. At the same time, he instinctively knew that God's wrath was real, that God's justice could not be nullified, that God's condemnation of sin was unabated. Surely it is ironic that, while Erskine so intensely stressed love as the fundamental attribute of God, he never challenged the implications of the biblical narrative of the Fall. Was the sin of Adam and Eve so monstrous that it brought God's curse on the whole of humankind? Or was God's punitive nature so merciless that even the slightest sin drew divine wrath down on us all? Erskine never addressed these questions directly, nor did he recognize the need to do so, given his basic assumptions. Surely his unceasing advocacy of the character of God should have led him to do more than he did. The result is that much of what he says in respect to the classically argued relation between God's mercy and God's justice is surprisingly naive, and often simplistic. He gave voice, for instance, to such commonplaces as "Love does not overstep or silence the claims of justice but meets and fulfills them" (Evidence, p. 77). Or, again: it is not a question of "love in the right hand and justice in the left," but a "love which hates, and seeks to eradicate sin" (Serpent, p. 24). What lay behind and beneath such sentiments was Erskine's abiding rejection, as one author has put it, of Calvinism's "emphasis on the sovereignty of God [which] had been tragically transformed at the hands of the dogmaticians who underscored God's power at the expense of the loving nature of that power."[14] It is no surprise, therefore, that it was in his *The Doctrine of Election* that he argued, albeit in an often inchoate and repetitious fashion, for a re-visioning or reinterpretation of the "received" doctrine of election. Erskine did himself admit that had once held to the Westminster theory of election, but added that he rather "submitted" to it than "believed" it (Election, p. 4). He went on to wrestle valiantly with some of the "dark passages" of Scripture, especially Romans 9 where it appears that the elect are saved and the reprobate damned. And, in one insightful passage, he did manage to spy out one of the major assumptions that lay behind the received doctrine:

> I believe that it is the fear of attributing glory to man in his own salvation, and of taking glory from God, that attaches many people to the doctrines of Calvinism, but they would do well to consider whether they are not, in fact, withholding from God the glory which

he desires in man and seeking to force upon Him a kind of glory which He does not desire (Election, p. 60).

Interestingly, Erskine came close to turning the whole system of election and reprobation on its head when he suggested that it not so much God but *we* who have the elective power. God does indeed choose and call all people, but men and women are free to choose, free to "elect" to refuse so free a gift. "Volition" and "cooperation," therefore, belong to the grammar of human responsibility. Or, as Erskine stated, "accepting the gift" is "our part of the work of salvation."

Erskine's experience and perception of God made it impossible to think in terms of arbitrary or vindictive justice. Yet God did and does punish, he believed; God did and does condemn. The sentence of death (which, as I said earlier, Erskine never questioned) has not been abrogated. Yet, in all this, it was God's will that *sin* be destroyed, not God's chosen people.[15] Only in filial trust, he said, could one welcome God's sentence upon sin; only by those afflictions sent by God could one shed one's God-denying self-will; only as one knows God as "Father" can one gladly accept corrections and judgments as God's way of making one happy and holy — forever! (Election, p. 338)

Erskine first articulated his understanding of educative punishment in his *The Unconditional Freeness of the Gospel*: "Sorrow," he wrote, "can be used to good purpose: "[I]t cannot restore man to the true vine but it gives pause to the soul, it shows that we are not able ourselves to help ourselves ... [I]t awakens a sense of need, and thus, by the Divine blessing, often becomes the instrument of drawing sinners back to God" (Freeness, pp. 18f). But "terror" or "fear" are not instruments of God's choosing. We are assured that God's purpose is "not to destroy but to correct; that is, not to inflict present suffering as retribution, but to train [us] into a participation in [God's] own holiness" (Freeness, p. 74). Curative and corrective sufferings: these are part of the human condition; they are also palpable testimony to God's abhorrence of sin.

Archibald Robertson, in his attack upon Erskine's "misrepresentation," did confess that the doctrine of election was hard for many people either to understand or to accept. The "natural" mind, he said, has a "bias" against so stern a doctrine; it was revolting to some; others felt it made God the author of sin; still others saw it as destroying the freedom of moral agancy, introducing "iron-handed Necessity, or Blind Destiny" to a fallen race.[16] Surely Erskine was of such a "natural" mind. And it was particularly in the writings of Jonathan Edwards (one of the few theologians whom he criticized by name) that Erskine experienced the "revulsion" of which Robertson spoke. Edwards, he wrote (in a pejorative tone), was a "theological metaphysician" who sought — vainly — to insist that the doctrine of election was not incompatible with human freedom. Erskine claimed that, for Edwards, humankind was in a state of utter helplessness, so much so that only an exterior power could save them. The Fall left men and women with no intrinsic or inherent good, no capacity even to recognize the good, let alone the ability to do the good. Not so for Erskine. Our own conscience, he believed, teaches us otherwise, namely, that our freedom consists of being so infused with God's Spirit that we are able to identify, and enter into, God's purposes for us, and therefore to embrace the good. Edwards' definition of freedom, wrote Erskine, was manifestly wrong; it was but an abstraction, with no reference to genuine human nature or to our relation to God — or to God's relation to us. Love it is that enables this relation; it is God's own love that grants us true freedom. Edwards, Erskine went on to say, "has not preached peace; [he] has preached perplexity and doubt, by declaring that the Father of Jesus Christ is not the father of all men — and that, though He created all men, He loves only a few of them (Election, p. 569).

How to explain, then, what the author of the Epistle to the Hebrews says of God's chastening? [W]hat son is he whom the Father chasteneth not? ... [If] ye be without chastisement, whereof all are partakers, then ye are bastards, and not sons" (Hebrews 12:7-8). Erskine was quick to quote a verse that follows: [God] afflicteth not willingly, but for *our* profit, that we may be partakers of his holiness" (*ibid.*, 12:10). Affliction, chastisement, chastening — these indeed are employed by our parental God, but out of concern for our growth in holiness. They are not vengeful visitations from on high. And Erskine's view here certainly is not merely a "spare the rod and spoil the child" approach. God's justice is not the enemy to be avoided at all costs; rather, it is both our friend and the "enemy of our enemy," i.e. sin (Sp. Order, pp.72f). Just as God's love is not to be misconstrued as an "easy benevolence," similarly God's justice is not to be construed as a "false tenderness." God takes our sin with utter seriousness. For this reason, God does not shrink from inflicting suffering so as to draw the sinner out from sin. Erskine enjoined his readers, as did the Psalmist, to "[s]ing unto the Lord, all ye saints of his, and give thanks at the remembrance of his holiness" (Sp. Order, p. 71).[17] One can but wonder whether Erskine assumed that his readers would automatically recall the next verse: "For his anger endureth but for a moment; in his favor is life: weeping may endure for a night, but joy cometh in the morning."

Erskine could, in fact, "sing unto the Lord," since he believed that God reaches out to all, providing all with a plan of education, by which our self-will might be overcome; with training, by which we might be drawn to God and emulate God's own righteousness; by testing, as a result of which we grow to acknowledge our need for, and dependence on, God. God's justice and mercy, therefore, are "remedial," "corrective," and "purposeful," in order that we may encounter in God, not the "cold eye" of a judge, but the "encouraging love" of a parent (Sp. Order, p. 65). "Terror," or abject "fear of God" renders "filial trust" impossible. And anything short of God's love robs the Gospel of its "healing virtue" (Sp. Order, 62f).

After a visit to Erskine at Linlathen, in November of 1865, Principal John Tulloch wrote to Robert H. Story:

> Our old friend here is full of spiritual wisdom as ever ... as he expounded and re-expounded his favorite idea of the spiritual education under which every man and the whole race are, and of God as a *teaching* Father ... All men are undergoing this education; but some — the most — are doing so unconsciously, feebly, scarcely at all. But all are yet destined to the full realisation of their spiritual state and dignity. The idea that punishment can be anything but a temporary phase of the divine dealing with man, for their good in the end, to mark His very love to them, in their deliverance from sin, seems to him now, from recent discussions, to be quite in the ascendant in the theological mind.[18]

"Love is the name of God." It is that conviction as to the abiding "character of God" that lay at the heart of Erskine's faith. It was a conviction not articulated as "doctrine," since Erskine's was a subjective, intuitive, and experiential faith, seldom, if ever, expressed in the language of the schools. His constant prayer, indeed as we have seen, was that he might "see, and hear, and feel" God in everything. And what he saw and heard and felt was that God's love was universal, expressed through mutual indwelling. It was an unceasingly inviting love. Too, it was a sacrificial, self-giving love, exercised at infinite cost. It was also an eternally patient love, so enduring as to know no temporal boundaries. And it was a purposeful love, making use of remedial and corrective measures so as to draw all people into one divine family. Erskine expressed all of this with passion and conviction, even if, at times, somewhat clumsily.

I have already mentioned (Ch. I, at n. 2) Dr. John Brown's poignant description of Erskine a few days before the latter's death in 1870. This present chapter, then, may aptly be concluded with a quotation alluded to above from a letter to Brown, written by Erskine, consoling his physician friend on the occasion of his wife's death. The letter is dated 7 January 1864.

> What a blessed and glorious thing human existence would be, if we fully realised that the infinitely wise and infinitely powerful God loves each one of us with an intensity infinitely beyond what the most fervid human spirit ever felt towards another, and with a concentration as if He had none else to think of!"[19]

CHAPTER SIX: THE CHARACTER OF GOD

Notes to Chapter Six

1. Erskine wrote of those "philosophers" and "teachers" who often conversed about God but for whom the word "God" was impressed on their minds only as a "logical datum."

2. Erskine used the term "notion," as did F.D. Maurice, to indicate a superficial or erroneous view, as distinct from "principle," i.e., an idea or concept grounded in reality. See Richard Norris, "Maurice on Theology," in McClain, Norris, and Orens, *F.D. Maurice: A Study* (Cambridge, MA: Cowley, 1982), pp. 3-21.

3. And Ewing himself observed that "too often theology is but a *hortus siccus* of dead plants, of which the learned collector has the lifeless form, the unlearned gardener the bloom and the beauty." *Address to Younger Clergy*, p. 27.

4. As to transubstantiation, the following quotation, simple and direct, makes Erskine's view clear beyond a doubt: "The consecration of the bread and wine cannot mean changing their nature, but simply using them in worship — using them according to the last instructions of our Lord, in remembrance of Him" (Hanna, p. 336). As to the "doctrine" of the Trinity, Erskine is somewhat evasive. "The abstract fact that there is a plurality in the unity of the Godhead really makes no address either to our understandings, or our feelings, or our consciences" (Evidence, p. 64). Earlier in the same volume Erskine confessed that "[t]he distinction between persons in the Divine nature we cannot comprehend," which statement led J.H. Newman to comment, quoting in fact from Erskine himself: "[It would appear that, for Erskine], Christianity holds out a premium for believing improbabilities." J.H. Newman, *Tracts for the Times*, No 73, p. 24. This is also quoted in John Tulloch, *Movements of Religious Thought in Britain*, p. 140.

5. Erskine's letter of 23 September 1867 to Ewing contains a further interpretation of this point.

6. Thomson, *The Doctrine of Universal Pardon*, pp. 485f. That Thomson, instead of using the word "God," was given to use such distant terms as "Supreme Being," "Divine Essence," or "Divinity," is perhaps an indication of why he found Erskine's "familiarity" so distasteful.

7. Robertson, *Vindication*, p. 175.

8. As noted above (Ch. 4 at n. 3), another critic complained of Erskine's "lamentable indecorum" in speaking of the immediate "presence of Deity" with "disgusting familiarity." Anon., *The Port-Glasgow Miracles*, pp. 25f.

9. The reference is to Isaiah 49:15.

10. Ewing has stressed this point: Erskine did not view love as an "easy benevolence that makes little of sin." God's love, for him, was "a most righteous love" (Ewing, IV.14). See also Sp. Order, pp. 233, 245.

11. This quotation comes from a letter to Edward Craig, written sometime in 1864.

12. Hebrews 13:5 and Isaiah 54:10.

13. Anon., *Examination and Refutation*, p. 14.

14. Steve Gowler, "No Second-Hand Religion," p. 212.

15 Too often, said Erskine, we are more concerned to "escape punishment" than to "become righteous." "[T]he life and death of Christ have come to be regarded as a propitiation to Divine justice through which mercy may be extended to the guilty, than as a manifestation of that righteousness which God desires to see in us, and of his righteous love, which, whilst it never ceases to condemn our sin, can never cease to seek our deliverance from sin" (Sp. Order, p. 64).

16 Robertson, *op. cit.*, p. 117. In spite of this acknowledgement, Robertson went on to say — predictably — that on such matters Scripture is "distinct and decided" (p. 78).

17 Psalm 30:4.

18 Margaret Oliphant, *A Memoir of the Life of John Tulloch, D.D., LL.D.* (Edinburgh, 1889; second edition), pp. 216f. It is not clear whether Tulloch agreed with Erskine here since he concluded this paragraph somewhat enigmatically: "What a cheerful, hopeful, yet pathetic confidence [Erskine] has!"

19 *Letters of Dr. John Brown*, p. 178.

CHAPTER SEVEN: ATONEMENT

> "We must not interpret the condemnation of our conscience as a declaration from God that He has cast us off, but rather as His declaration that, because He has *not* cast us off, He cannot permit us to go on separating ourselves from Him. (Sp. Order, p. 153).

In the Preface to this study (and also at the end of Chapter Four), I stated that Erskine "was happily not without his faults, nor his writings without their inconsistencies and egregious errors." I must say at this point that I have to omit the work "happily," for egregious errors there are, as well as passages that are "ill-considered and naive." So lest my presentation of Erskine's theological posture develop into an uncritical panegyric, I need now to present some of these inconsistencies and errors. This chapter, then, will take a critical turn as I examine points of doctrine in Erskine's writings that demand our attention.

Many of his writings were indeed pilloried as contrary to Westminster orthodoxy, or as unbiblical, or as an idiosyncratic venture into the theological enterprise by an untutored "layman." The reasons for such criticisms are eminently clear. Erskine's championing of the doctrines of universal salvation and of personal assurance was bound to elicit negative responses, given the theological tenor of his day. Erskine, as we have seen, was attacked (and Campbell deposed), but in spite of this he never tired of promulgating with an uncommon combination of passion and commitment these his favorite doctrines. "It is striking," he wrote somewhat wistfully, "that the *universal atonement* and the *personal assurance* should have been a reproach at all times" (Serpent, p. 170). Inasmuch as he held tenaciously to these doctrines, it is not surprising that, of all the major traditional doctrines of the Christian faith, it was, by his own admission, the doctrine of atonement that was central to his thought. Nor is it surprising that John Henry Newman, presumably voicing the Tractarians' emphasis on the Incarnation, accused Erskine of presumptuousness precisely on this point.[1] For Newman to claim (as did Erskine) that "the doctrine of atonement [was] the cornerstone of Christianity ... to which all other doctrines of revelation are subservient" was an outrageous position.[2] Not so for Erskine. In an even stronger statement than that quoted by Newman, Erskine insisted that the "doctrine of atonement is the great subject of revelation. God is represented as delighting in it, as being glorified by it, [and] as being most fully manifested by it. All other doctrines radiate from this as their centre." (Evidence, p. 68).

Among nineteenth-century British Protestants, no doctrine received as much attention as did the atonement; countless pamphlets, articles, and book-length treatises were devoted to a seemingly infinite variety of interpretations of this doctrine. The majority of these (especially from those of an "evangelical" persuasion) tended to restate or argue for the importance of the so-called "Latin" or "Penal Substitution" theory of the atonement which had its classical exposition centuries ago in Anselm's *Cur Deus Homo*? At the forefront of many of these arguments were questions which had to do with the "extent" of the atonement (limited or universal?), with the relationship between God's "justice" and God's "mercy," and with what might be called the "mechanics" of atonement (how effected). And ever-present in this literature was the christological question: Who is Jesus Christ and what is (was) his role in the work of salvation?

It is difficult — perhaps even impossible — to place Erskine and his views on the wide spectrum of atonement theories. Surely he found some of them harsh (i.e., denying the loving character of God), others of them too "transactional" (i.e., so much punishment for so much sin), and a few of them embroiled in the "metaphysical subtleties of the schools." Surely, too, he could not subscribe to any view that interpreted Christ's death exclusively as a requisite payment to God so as to appease God's wrath and/or satisfy the divine honour. Yet it is here, initially, that one can discern a flaw in Erskine's approach. It seems that he was able to point out those views with which he disagreed; less able, however, to articulate his own view with any clarity or consistency. This stems in large degree from his wildly random use of technical terms, many of them directly associated with those theories of which he was critical: transaction, vindication, substitution, satisfaction, etc. Such terminological myopia may, in fact, have been due to Erskine's relative unfamiliarity with the history and development of atonement theory; it may also be due to his constant habit of relying exclusively on Hebrew and Christian Scriptures to support his position, for in the Bible — especially in the New Testament — the vocabulary associated with salvation is diverse in the extreme and therefore subject to diverse interpretations. Two examples from his writings may be illustrative of his rather "loose" use of technical terms.

> [Christ's sufferings] were not only endured in *satisfaction* of the Divine *justice*, — they also serve as a pattern of the way by which God leads those real sinners whom the sinless Saviour represented unto holiness. (Evidence, p. 114)[3]

> The *judicial* sentence against sin has been executed, and the *honor* of the Divine law has been *vindicated* by a deed of unutterable love ... The belief of this *transaction* [changes] the heart into conformity with the love of God. (Evidence, p. 117)[4]

Further, Erskine was more than once quite explicit in his assertion that "Christ hath redeemed us from the condemnation of the law, having endured that condemnation in our stead" (Evidence, p. 136), a view which, as we shall see, is totally at odds with what he wrote in his later books.

Apart from this palpably un-systematic lack of terminological precision (including, it seems a lack of awareness of the implications of his rather haphazard vocabulary), a further serious difficulty presents itself. Given the centrality of the atonement to his thought, and given a certain clarity as to those views which he was unwilling to accept, the images which Erskine employed to represent his views are highly intuitive, often fanciful, and engagingly metaphorical, so much so as to be misleading. Concrete, rational expression was not one of Erskine's gifts. Here are but two short examples. "No creative mind," he wrote, "can receive a full impression of the Divine character, — the highest archangel cannot look upon the cross of Christ as God looks upon it, — how much less can man, who is a worm!" (Faith, p. 50) Or again: "Christianity may be considered as a divinely revealed system of medical treatment for diseased spirits. Heaven is the name for health in the soul and Hell is the name for the disease; and the design of Christianity is to produce heaven and to destroy hell" (Freeness, p. 3).[5] This penchant for metaphor reaches its rhetorical height in this imaginative assertion: "It is the genial ray of the Sun [sic] of righteousness, and not the storm of divine wrath, which compels the sinner to lay down the weapons of his rebellion" (Baxter, p. x). Such flights of fancy, I believe, have the tendency on occasion seriously to detract from one's capacity to comprehend the content and contours of Erskine's atonement theory, although his obvious enthusiasm and highly affective prose may be commended.

Perhaps the most problematic of Erskine's errors, not touched upon by any of his contemporary critics (nor, as far as I know, by any subsequent interpreters of his theology), has to do with his understanding of God's condemnation of sin. In the previous chapter I suggested that God's "chastening" or "afflictions" were, for Erskine, neither arbitrary nor vindictive; rather they were corrective, educative, purposeful, and remedial, and therefore consonant with the loving character of God. These sentiments, on Erskine's part, were articulated largely in response to the received doctrine of election. But, when Erskine wrote of God's condemnation of sin within the context of his atonement theory, a less comforting picture emerges. For all his sustained insistence on the universality of pardon, a close reading of Erskine's works reveals that there was in his mind some doubt or question as to what had in fact been accomplished by the death of Christ. On the one hand, he saw Christ's sacrifice as freeing humankind from the bondage of sin; on the other hand, he was quite clear in his assertion that men and women, due to their sinful nature, continue to stand under the penalty of God's righteous condemnation. Did Erskine equivocate in this regard, or is it yet another example — and a very telling example — of his lack of theological precision? Perhaps both.

In 1822 Erskine wrote that because Christ suffered the punishment we sinners deserved, pardon has been universally bestowed; this act of "amnesty," he went on to say, is in fact "antecedent to our belief, and independent of it ... though we scout it and reject it" (Evidence, p. 110). Then this observation:

The sentence has been executed, and the records of heaven bear testimony that "it is finished." The Divine gracious determination to pardon sinners through Christ is freely and universally proclaimed as an act already passed ..." (Faith, p. 112).

However, just a few years later, in 1828, Erskine had this to say: "Salvation does not consist in the removal of punishment, but in the willing acceptance of it" (Freeness, p. 120). More than this, the suffering and death of Christ are the suffering and death that all persons are to experience. Pardon, yes; removal of penalty, no.

These rather paradoxical, if not contradictory, statements appear with increased frequency in Erskine's writings, a clue to which can be seen in the subtitle of his *The Brazen Serpent*, namely, "Life Coming Through Death." Christ did not rise to life before he suffered death as the righteous sentence of God. Similarly, God has not dispensed with our need to suffer and die; rather than dispense with our suffering, God's intention was to "change the character of our suffering from an unsanctified and unsanctifying suffering [!]" (Serpent, p. 44). In other words, "Christ suffered so as to enable us to suffer, *as* he did, to the glory of God, and to the purification of our nature" (Serpent, p. 55). Whose was the more salvific suffering? we might ask — Christ's or ours?

Erskine may himself have been aware of some of the less happy implications of his views. "Let me not be misunderstood," he wrote, "when I say that the furnace is necessary to purge away our sins, as if I said that the atonement of Christ was incomplete, and that any affliction on our part is necessary to complete it" (Serpent, p. 62). Yet even his assertion just a few pages later that Christ's sacrifice "was done *once for all* [and that] *no more is required*" (Serpent, p. 90) does not dispel the "misunderstanding" to which Erskine's views were bound to give rise. Nor does his quotation from the Book of Daniel help much: "He hath finished transgression, and made an end of sin, and made reconciliation for iniquity, and brought in an everlasting righteousness."[6] But clearly, for Erskine, transgression and sin and iniquity abide, as does the punishment due them.

There is a profound irony here. Erskine could claim unequivocally that the doctrine of atonement was absolutely central to the Christian revelation, yet nowhere else than in his attempted delineation of this specific doctrine was he as inchoate and confusing (at best) or as contradictory and dissembling (at worst). And this cannot be due solely to his lack of terminological precision or to his excessive use of metaphor. His whole understanding of the relationship between condemnation and pardon, penalty and forgiveness is absolutely at odds with his conviction as to the universality of salvation. There is, however, one aspect of his atonement theory where Erskine did achieve a certain amount of clarity and coherence (yet still not without its difficulties). This has to do with his understanding of the word "substitution" as it appears frequently in atonement theories of the day, and a word often associated with the Latin (or "penal substitution") theory. Although he did, as we have seen, employ this concept in his earlier writings, he later found it to be unacceptable. In 1822 he wrote that "God gave his equal and well-beloved Son to suffer *in the stead* of an apostate world" (Evidence, p. 50). In 1831, however, he retreated from this view, pointing out that the current common perception was that "Christ came to save sinners, and that he could accomplish this only by suffering in their stead the punishment due their sin" (Serpent, p. 40), going on to aver that this is a "very defective view, to say the least of it" (Serpent, p. 41). His point was driven home with some force, as seen in the following quotation.

> The humanly devised doctrine of substitution has come in the place of, and has cast out, the true doctrine of the headship of Christ, which is the large and glorious and true explanation of these passages of Scripture which are commonly interpreted as teaching substitution. (Serpent, pp. 41f)

> The blood of bulls and goats could never take away sin ... because they were *substitutes*; their blood was not the blood of the offender. (Serpent, p. 42)[7]

Rather than being a "substitute," thought Erskine, Christ is our "Head," our "Representative," and our "Leader." Substitution, he wrote, as if to clinch his argument, is not a biblical word![8]

Alexander Ewing, in many respects not only a friend and admirer of Erskine, but also a promulgator of his views, was equally convinced as to the theological inappropriateness of the substitution theory. He said that atonement

> is bringing nigh of God and man, a deliverance, a redemption, a restoration of man. It is a work having for its object the conformity of the human nature to the divine ... No substitution could do this.[9]

Erskine's rejection of the substitution theory led him, if nothing else, to state his views on the atonement with greater consistency and clarity than usual. It led him also to temper his exaggerated and often overwrought use of metaphor. Yet a further examination of his position reveals that his criticism of the substitution theory is quite different from most of the objections raised against it by liberal theologians — and those objections were indeed many. Most of them arose out of the strong dissatisfaction with any view that portrays a God who inflicts punishment at all, whether on an obedient and innocent victim in our stead or on the human race as a whole. Erskine's objections were not these. He said, and seemingly never tired of saying, that the suffering and death of Christ in no way abrogated the suffering and death visited by God on humankind. It was for this reason, in Erskine's mind, that Christ *could not be our substitute*. Put rather simplistically, if Christ is the Head of the human race, and if we humans are branches grafted into his root, then it appears that Christ did not suffer *for* us (substitution) but *in* us (participation). And we in him.

It may be within the context of Erskine's rather idiosyncratic christology, then, that it is possible to discern how it was that he could advocate God's pardon and forgiveness as a universal reality ("Would it not be a blessed relief to be assured that Christ died, not for believers, but for the world ...?" [Freeness, p. 79]) while at the same time claiming that the human race remained under the condemnation of God:

> Christ was wounded for our transgressions and bruised for our iniquities [cf. Isaiah 53:5]. And thus in the very root of [our human] nature, he put the mark of hatred and condemnation on every form of human sin. (Serpent, p. 52)

Even more explicitly:

> Why was the suffering of our nature in the person of Jesus needful? It was a *fallen* nature; a nature which had fallen by sin; and which, in consequence of this, lay under condemnation. (Serpent, pp. 37f)

In spite of his assertion, variously stated, that it was God who "bruised" Christ, Erskine did not want the death of Jesus to be interpreted as a "judicial" act on the part of God; nor was Christ's to be understood as a "vicarious" death; the atonement, he claimed, was neither a "forensic" or "legalistic" exchange. And the doctrine of "expiation" he criticized as a "human invention" (Sp. Order, p. 151). It appears that Erskine gradually became more and more wary of terminology that was associated with the Latin theory of atonement. Yet if atonement could not be described by such words or concepts, how can one speak of it? How can one characterize Christ's patient and obedient submission to divine affliction? Erskine sought valiantly to persuade his readers that the cross was a work of love: not the "punishment of a Judge" but the chastisement of a tender "Father" (Hanna, p. 216). Christ's suffering (and our suffering in him) were indeed "penal" (Erskine did continue to use this term), but given and received in a "spirit of holy love" (Serpent, p. 53).[10]

The patent inconsistency or incongruity of such statements, when placed alongside Erskine's universalism, may to some extent be ameliorated by his understanding, touched upon in the previous chapter, that God is not only the afflicter but the afflicted as well. God's love is a patient, grieving, and wounded love. And it is here that I find Erskine's christology most powerfully articulated. What he said on this point, in one of his earliest books, is noteworthy:

> God has presented himself even to our senses, clothed in our nature, walking and conversing as a man among men, fulfilling all the offices and all the sorrows of life, that we might think of him not only with terror and strangeness, but even with respectful confidence and intimacy. (Faith, p. 82)

And in a later work Erskine was able to describe God's participation in the death of Christ in this manner:

> We are in God's hands ... [W]hilst we think him a stern Judge, or a severe task-master, his hand appears a prison to us ... but as soon as we discover the print of the nail in his hand, then that which had been a terror or a wilderness to us ... we find to be in fact a city of securest and sweetest refuge. (Serpent, p. 33)

As must be clear from these references to Erskine's works, the major portion of his doctrine of atonement is to be found in Chapter II of his *The Brazen Serpent*, entitled "Christ the Head." To read this chapter, as we have seen, is to find oneself immersed in a series of theological dissonances: powerful affirmations as to the loving participation of God in Christ's suffering appear side-by-side with pronouncements as to God's punitive wrath. And this dissonance is heightened by the wondrous variety of ways in which Erskine sought to denominate Christ in relation to God. He seems to have subscribed to some extent to traditional orthodoxy in his claim that Jesus was "God Incarnate" or even "the second person in the Godhead" (Serpent, p. 67). In almost the same breath, however, he spoke of Christ as God in our nature, as Jehovah in the flesh, or the "union of Jehovah with our fallen flesh" (Serpent, p. 149). Christ is also our "mighty God" (see below). Clearly Erskine was not over concerned with the niceties of christological doctrine.[11] He did, however, stress the "divinity" of Christ: "If Jesus was merely a man, [then] the greatest part of the Bible is mere bombast" (Evidence, p. 91). And Erskine could also, with equal stress, affirm the "humanity" of Jesus, albeit somewhat ambiguously: "[T]he human nature of Jesus Christ is just an exposition of the manner of God's love to every man" (Serpent, p. 125). What he was to write later (15 January 1861) to Bishop Ewing is considerably clearer:

> Jesus Christ was truly a man, and truly tempted ... He came into humanity and went through the education of humanity, laying down self at each step. He would not have been a real man if he had not had that self in him which would seek its own. ... Unless Christ was truly a man, there was no revelation of the Father through Him to us. (Ewing, I.27f)

A comparison of the following two quotations may further serve to illustrate Erskine's multi-faceted christological posture, and serve also to underline the "dissonance" between his view of God's punitive disposition and God's sacrificial love:

> When we contemplate the Son of Man lifted up on the cross, we see in him the Son of God, in our very nature, suffering by his own will and by the infliction of the Father, the whole curse denounced against sin — sorrow and death — that thus he might ... become the righteous channel of divine favour ... [Then] we see a glorious manifestation ... of God's love. (Serpent, p. 39)

> The great truth with regard to the sacrifice [of the cross] is that Christ is in the flesh of every man, and that by its shedding, every man's sin hath been condemned and put away ... (Serpent, p. 148)

The atonement may very well have been central to Erskine's theology, but surely his attempts to explain it were not successful. Much of what he wrote was naive; some of it contradictory; and, I suspect, portions of it theologically untenable. (As to whether or not these are "egregious errors" I will leave the reader to judge.) Fortunately, there are occasional passages to be found in Erskine's writings where his advocacy for the loving character of God is stated in such a way as to transcend his often tortured explications of the atonement. This passage, for instance, sheds more light than gloom:

> This very Christ, the glorious hope of the world, is in your flesh, and in him you have eternal life. Reader, however overlooked by God you may think yourself, and lost in the mass of mankind, — however excluded you may think yourself from his mercy, — however polluted and defiled and corrupted you may know yourself to be, — however vain and futile you have hitherto found your attempts to meet the demands of your own conscience, — this is the message of God to you. You have in your flesh him who is the righteous head, on whose account sin is not imputed to you, and who is the mighty God, in whose strength you may overcome all the evil that is in you. (Serpent, pp. 166f)[12]

One cannot but wonder whether or not Erskine himself was dissatisfied with this attempted interpretation of the doctrine of atonement, whether or not he discerned in it an awkward and ill-fitting juxtaposition to his universalism, and whether or not he was aware of the implications of his statement that "[t]here are those who seek salvation *from* the cross," but God's salvation is "*through* the cross" (Serpent, p. 49).[13] It may be, as we have already seen, that Erskine wrote no more books after the publication of *The Doctrine of Election* because he was tired of controversy or, as some of his letters suggest, that in many respects his mind had changed or that he came to be less than pleased with some of what he had written. Apart from his own characteristic self-doubts,[14] there is insufficient evidence to explain his withdrawal from writing. There is evidence, however, that many of Erskine's harsher views were in his later years considerably softened. The papers and fragments collected and published posthumously under the title *The Spiritual Order*, as well as his considerable correspondence, indicate that much of what he had written earlier was no longer of consuming interest to him. The "Brazen Serpent" had lost, if not its sheen, certainly its symbolic power. And his often extravagant depiction of the person and work of Christ was radically simplified. In a little essay entitled "The Divine Son," one finds an orderly, consistent, and coherently articulated christology (and one, I suspect, which was unique to Erskine) that is a far cry from his previous rhetorical untidiness and theological prolixity. Clearly he had left behind him his often ill-fated forays into the arena of theological argumentation. Erskine, as we have seen, was not given to speculations about the doctrine of the Trinity, so there is no cause for surprise that this little essay is unabashedly binitarian (the Holy Spirit is not mentioned once!).[15] His position may be summarized as follows.

The "doctrine" of God's fatherly relation to, and purposes for, all of humankind has been fully revealed in Christ. All other doctrines are explanatory and corroborative of this fundamental principle. The "divinity" of Jesus indicates that within the Divine nature there must be a distinction analogous to the relationship between Father and Son. This Erskine called the "principle of reciprocity." The terms which best illustrate this principle are those of giving and receiving, of paternal trustworthiness and filial trust, or of ruling rightly and obeying rightly.

> For every form of goodness in God there is a corresponding recipient form; consequently ... there must be in the Divine nature distinct personalities representing these two forms, otherwise there could be no possibility either of their exercise or of their manifestation. (p. 35)

Erskine went on to speak of "two hemispheres" in the Divine nature, the one upper and the other lower, or the one active and the other passive. It was thus possible for him to hold together what might otherwise be "scarcely intelligible," namely the claim made by Jesus that "I and the Father are one" *and* "My Father is greater than I." This suggests that there is also a superior (divine) and inferior (human) relationship within the Godhead. Accordingly, Erskine could go on to say that the divine/human "unity" consists not in "singleness" but in "completeness," that is, there can be no revelation of Fatherhood apart from a revelation of Sonship. Fatherhood, in fact, would be but an "honorary title" were we not to realize, further, that *we* are created in the Son and therefore are "actual partakers with him in the filial relationship to his and our Father" (p. 38, n. 1). Humankind, then, participates in the principle of reciprocity: every man and woman is a child of God. We can therefore welcome Christ as our "Mediator" and "Daysman" since he partakes "both of the nature of Him from whom we have been alienating ourselves, and of our own, and in whom — the true Son of Man — we may draw near to the Father" (p. 41).

If one compares the convoluted argumentation found in *The Brazen Serpent* to "The Divine Son," the latter has a lightness and gentleness and freshness and simplicity that makes it a delight to read, whether or not one agrees with the specifics of Erskine's presentation. And, happily, Erskine did not include in his principle of reciprocity the two hemispheres of punisher/punished (as otherwise might have been expected). Yet Erskine, for all the softening of previously held positions, did not abandon his conviction that "the sentence of sorrow and death is not to be set aside," although he iterated this more in a context of hope than of despair. In two small fragments appearing towards the end of *The Spiritual Order*, he wrote: "And this is the character of Christian faith; it is faith in God who led his Son *through* death into new life" (Sp. Order, p. 252). Sorrow and death, then, do not have the last word.

> The Father sent the Son [wrote Erskine] to pass through man's suffering and death to prove that whilst He saw it to be right and inevitable that sin should be visited by sorrow and death, His love ceases not to rest on those thus visited; and that it was therefore their right and duty to trust that love throughout the whole process. (Sp. Order, p. 253)[16]

In reflecting on Erskine's understanding of atonement and salvation, it does seem possible, in spite of the criticisms I have expressed, to separate the tares from the wheat in Erskine's theological garden. Let me conclude this chapter, then by pointing to two positive elements within his atonement theory that I believe are worthy of attention. The first is this. For Erskine the revelation of God in Jesus Christ was not exclusively limited to historical events. Christ's life, death, and resurrection, that is, were indeed events within space and time, but they were also a manifestation of what has always been true and always will be true of the character of God, and especially true of God's relation to humankind. "The appearance of Jesus Christ on earth," wrote Erskine, was "the expression of an infinite love already existing in the Father's heart" (Sp. Order, p. 152). That is why the Laird of Linlathen could speak of salvation, not merely as something to be hoped for in the future but as a present reality, a present possession. As I pointed out earlier, one of Erskine's favorite biblical texts was John 17:3 — "And this is life eternal that they might know the only true God and Jesus Christ whom thou hast sent." The present tense — "is" — was important to Erskine, since his thought patterns were not always linear; rather, he could speak as if the past and the future were to be discovered in the "now" of human experience. He believed it to be a serious misconception to think of salvation as "not yet."

> Salvation ... cannot be a thing of place or time; in its essence it must be the same here and hereafter; and it follows that the idea of having heaven without holiness is like the idea of having health without being well. (Freeness, pp. 3f)

Related to this first point is a second, namely, one having to do with Erskine's conception of "eternal." Referring to John 17:3, he commented: "Eternal life is not given as a premium for knowing God; the knowledge of God as revealed in Jesus Christ *is eternal life*" (Freeness, p. 108). To know God and to be known by God, to live into God and to receive God into one's self, this is to partake of life eternal. "This," he wrote, "I conceive is salvation; I don't understand any other meaning of salvation" (Hanna, p. 417). And in a letter to Edward Craig, Erskine had this to say:

> I don't believe that *aionios*, the Greek word rendered "eternal" and "everlasting" by our translators, really has that meaning. I believe that it refers to a man's essential spiritual state, and not to time, either finite or infinite. Eternal life is living in the love of God; eternal death is living in self. (Hanna, p. 425)[17]

Heaven, therefore, is not a place; nor is it a future reward. Similarly, hell is not a place; nor is it a future punishment. Heaven and hell are both states of present relationship to God. And, Erskine urged, God is the one in whom to live is life eternal. He urged even more insistently that God's patience knows no limits and that those who may now be out of relation with God, who are presently alienated from God, these God will soon woo into the divine family.[18]

So I end this chapter on a positive note, bringing us back to Erskine's abiding conviction as to the universality of salvation. In spite of the force of some of my criticisms of his atonement theory, I believe this abiding conviction was in no way and at no time abrogated or diminished by what I have referred to as Erskine's egregious theological errors. That these errors did not prevent so careful a theologian as Frederick Denison Maurice from being powerfully influenced by Erskine's writings (as well as by his friendship) is, I trust, a case in point.[19]

Notes to Chapter Seven

1. Newman, *Tracts for the Times*, No. 73 (1836), p. 27.
2. Newman, *op. cit.* He is quoting here directly from Erskine, Evidence, p. 65.
3. See also Gambold, p. xi.
4. The italics in each of these two passages have been added.
5. Erskine's understanding of heaven and hell as "present states" have been touched upon (Ch. I at n. 4) and will be discussed below.
6. This is in fact a *mis*quotation from Daniel 9:4 and is taken totally out of context.
7. See also Election, pp. 250f: "The Jewish sacrifices were inefficient, *because they were substitutes*... My dear reader, Jesus is not a substitute for man, but the head of man."
8. Serpent, pp. 45, 176, 279; Election, p. 250, &c.
9. Ewing, *An Address to the Younger Clergy*, pp. 76f. Ralph Wardlaw was one of the several Scottish theologians who held an opposing view: "[I]t would be far more consistent to renounce the authority of the Bible at once, than to admit that authority, and deny that it teaches the doctrine of redemption by substitutionary sufferings or sacrificial atonement." *Discourses on the Nature and Extent of the Atonement of Christ* (1843), p. 26.
10. Similarly: [T]he cross declares [God's] love; this love crucifies those whom it loves" (Serpent, p. 285).
11. Steve Gowler's observation as to Erskine's lack of theological training is apt: Because he was independent of church parties and because his reading of theology was limited, Erskine was a "theological outsider." "No Second-hand Religion," p. 203. John Tulloch's observation is sharper: "What is most remarkable to a student now-a-days [1885] in both [Andrew Thomson and Thomas Erskine] is the lack of historical knowledge dealing with Christian dogma. Mr. Erskine is perhaps more deficient in this respect than his opponent." *Movements of Religious Thought in Britain*, p. 143.
12. I find it interesting that Erskine used a term here ("impute") which he had previously said to be a bad translation of the Greek.
13. Similarly: "We are all on the cross; let us remember that it is the appointed way to paradise when accepted as the righteous love of God" (Election, pp. 51f).
14. See Ch. IV at nn. 20-23.
15. In a footnote (p. 31) Erskine praised Richard H. Hutton's "The Incarnation and Principles of Evidence" (*Tracts for Priests and People*, xix, London, 1862), stating his pleasure that both Hutton and he (in "The Divine Son") had been led independently to the same conclusions.
16. When I first read this paragraph, the cry from Job 13:15 came not surprisingly to mind: "Though he slay me, yet will I trust him."
17. The implications of this for soteriology will be discussed in the next chapter.
18. John Tulloch, among others, has drawn our attention to Erskine's understanding of heaven as properly the name for a state in which one is conformed to the will of God.

[19] Robert Story was also one who could discern the wheat among the tares in Erskine's atonement theory: Several people, he noted, "fought against an austerely limited atonement, and formally forensic explanations of its relation to mankind ... Neither the Puritan scheme of salvation nor the so-called 'rectoral' hypothesis which saw Christ's suffering and death as an exhibition of divine justice and vindication of God's character as moral governor of the world" were satisfactory to their deepening spiritual consciousness. "The earliest and in some respects the most deeply spiritual and original representative of this unrest and wider outlook was a layman, Thomas Erskine of Linlathan." R.H. Story, *The Apostolic Ministry of the Scottish Church*, p. 307.

CHAPTER EIGHT: ERSKINE AND F.D. MAURICE

> According to C.R. Sanders, and indeed to Maurice himself, the greatest single influence on him was Samuel Taylor Coleridge.[1]
>
> Erskine seems to have made a deeper impression on Maurice's theology than any of his contemporaries.[2]

For any theologian there are countless acknowledged, unacknowledged, and, more often, unknown influences that have given shape to his or her thought-patterns, conceptual framework, or ideological commitments. Such influences are clearly so manifold and so varied that it is impossible to assert that one is more prevalent than another. It is, however, true that both Coleridge and Erskine were major figures in the development of Maurice's ideas; he acknowledged his indebtedness to each.[3] It is also important to note, especially given the nature of Maurice's bold anti-clericalism, that both Coleridge and Erskine were *laymen*.

Frederick Denison Maurice's first exposure to the influence of Erskine came at an early age. He had originally intended to read divinity at university, but, largely due to the denominational diversity, bickerings, and disputes within his family, he changed his mind and decided to read law instead. While staying in London prior to going up to Cambridge, he wrote a letter to a certain Lucy, a friend of his mother's.[4] In his letter, written one might suppose out of adolescent ambivalence, the following rather gloomy sentence appears: "[I feel myself] a being destined to a few short years of misery here, as an earnest of and preparation for that more enduring state of wretchedness and woe [in the hereafter]."[5] Lucy did not see fit to countenance such abject self-pity. She wrote back:

> Where is your authority for regarding any individual of the human race as *destined* to misery either here of hereafter? Such a view is not supported by the letter or the spirit of that revelation which alone can be admitted as evidence in the case.[6]

According to Maurice's son (and biographer), Lucy went on to say that any view which sees men and women destined to misery makes of God a pitiless tyrant and certainly not a God of love. Further, it turns out that "Dear Lucy" (as Maurice's mother called her) was a close "personal friend of Mr. Erskine of Linlathen ... [whose] books at this time were just beginning to appear ... and at the moment [she was] very much under his influence."[7]

It was later (in 1831) that Maurice formed a friendship with a Mr. Bruce (then a university undergraduate and later to become Lord Elgin, Governor-General of India), and it was through him that Maurice "became acquainted with the 'Brazen

Serpent' which produced a very important effect upon his mind."[8] Shortly thereafter he wrote to his sister Priscilla:

> I cannot ... give up Mr. Erskine, one of whose books has been unspeakably comfortable to me ... The peculiarities of his system may be true or not, but I am certain a light has fallen through him on the Scriptures which I hope I shall never lose.[9]

It is difficult to ascertain when Erskine and Maurice first actually met, but it does seem clear that they corresponded with each other from probably the mid-1830s. It is also eminently clear that their appreciation of each other's views, as well as their influence upon each other, grew from an early date. In an autobiographical sketch written to his son in 1870, Maurice reflected upon the beginnings of his friendship with Erskine:

> More and more I was led to ask myself what a Gospel to mankind must be; whether it must not have some other ground than the fall of Adam and the sinful nature of man. I had [been] helped much in finding an answer to this question by your dear old friend Mr. Erskine's books — and by the sermons of Mr. Campbell.[10]

In a letter to his sister, Mrs. Charles Stirling, written in 1838, Erskine in his turn spoke of his nascent relationship with Maurice, and of what may very well have been their first meeting: "[I visited with some young men and with] Maurice, who is a very metaphysical man; I have not got into him yet; I hope, when I return to London, to know him better" (Hanna, p. 198). One can only hope that Erskine's use of the term "metaphysical" was in this instance meant in a kindly way![11]

As indicated in the passage quoted from Maurice's autobiographical sketch of 1870, the question as to what a "Gospel to mankind" must be was central to his thought, and it was in dedicating his *The Prophets and Kings of the Old Testament* to Erskine that Maurice elucidated this view most forcefully. Maurice wrote the Epistle Dedicatory without telling Erskine of it beforehand; he did, however, write him a letter of apology for having taken so "great a liberty with [his] name," going on to say how he "wished to tell others of how much they as well as I owe to your books; how they seem to me to mark a crisis in the theological movements of the time."[12] Portions of the Dedication itself read as follows:

> Have we a Gospel for men, for all men? Is it a Gospel that God's will is a will to all good, a will to deliver them from all evil? Is it a Gospel that He has reconciled the world unto Himself? Is it this absolutely, or this with a multitude of reservations, explanations, contradictions?

It is more than twenty years since a book of yours brought home to my mind the conviction that no Gospel but this can be of use to the world, and that the Gospel of Jesus Christ is such a one.

Many of my conclusions may differ widely from those into which you have been led: I should be grieved to make you responsible for them. But I have tried in these sermons to shew that the story of the Prophets and the Kings of the Old Testament is as directly applicable to the modern world as any Covenanters ever dreamed, — but that it is applicable because it is a continual witness for a God of Righteousness, not only against idolatry but against that notion of a mere Sovereign Baal or Bel which underlies all idolatry, all tyranny, all immorality; I may claim you as [these sermons'] spiritual progenitor. You will see that they do bear a witness, though a feeble one, for a truth upon the acknowledgement of which I believe the well being of your land, and of ours, depends. You will pray that more courageous and faithful champions of it may be raised up [to demonstrate] that there is a Spirit of Love working in the hearts of human beings, and that the lives of those who submit to it are illuminated and transfigured by it.[13]

It was in the same year in which *The Prophets and Kings* was published that Maurice's best known and most controversial volume appeared: his *Theological Essays*. And it was this volume, because of its explicit universalism, that elicited from many quarters an outrage similar to that which greeted Erskine's writings in the 1820s and 30s. It was the concluding essay in the book ("Eternal Life and Eternal Death") that drew the sharpest criticisms. Parallel to Erskine's assertion that "He who waited so long for the formation of a piece of old red sandstone will surely wait with much long-suffering for the perfecting of a human spirit" was Maurice's unequivocal statement:

I ask no one to pronounce, for I dare not pronounce myself, what are the possibilities of resistance in a human will to the loving will of God. There are times when they seem to me — thinking of myself more than others — almost infinite. But I know that there is something which must be infinite. I am obliged to believe in an abyss of love which is deeper than the abyss of death: I dare not lose faith in that love.[14]

In the same essay Maurice argued, as had Erskine, that the word *aionios* is not to be construed as a durational term; it was, rather, a concept descriptive of relationship: "The state of eternal life and eternal death is not one we can refer only to the future, or that we can in any wise identify with the future."[15] Again, Maurice pointed to the absurdity of believing that God "has created multitudes whom He means to perish for ever and ever."[16] Similarly, he inveighed against the "tendency throughout the history of the Church to determine the limits of God's love to men, and to speak of all but a few as hopelessly lost."[17]

The strenuous challenge to the current orthodoxy that the *Theological Essays* represented unleashed a torrent of often vitriolic rejoinders. The story of the events which led inexorably to Maurice's loss of his professorship at King's College, University of London, is a familiar one. Responding to pressure from outside the college as well as from within, it was as much a foregone conclusion that Maurice would be charged with heresy as it was in the case of John McLeod Campbell some two decades previously. Maurice himself indicated that he was not surprised at the outcome:

> The Council [of King's College] has pronounced that the opinions expressed and the doubts indicated in my Essays and in my correspondence respecting future punishment and the final issues of the day of judgment are of a dangerous tendency, and likely to unsettle the minds of theological students. They have decided further, that my continuance as Professor would be seriously detrimental to the interests of the College. The Principal [Dr. Jelf], acting as interpreter of the mind of the Council, has decreed that from the day on which its meeting was held, my Lectures, in both departments of the College, should cease.[18]

Some of the criticisms directed against Maurice were of a narrowly philosophic nature (such as H.L. Mansel's *Man's Conception of Eternity: An Examination of Mr. Maurice's Theory of a Fixed State out of Time* [19]), but the majority of them were aimed at Maurice's "heresy" of universalism. The *Theological Essays* produced what one commentator has described as a "theological maelstrom,"[20] one example of which is J.B. Mozley's response:

> Many statements and arguments in this [last] chapter appear to us not only highly dangerous, but positively unsound, and opposed to the doctrine of the Atonement as revealed in Scripture and always [*sic*] understood in the Church.[21]

Yet, as with the attacks made upon Erskine, behind the cries of "heresy!" and behind the noble attempts to preserve and safe-guard "orthodoxy," there were some observable, but often disguised, reasons for the virulence of the attacks made against Maurice. One of the more obvious found its source in a prevalent clerical elitism. Not only were Maurice's views likely to "unsettle the minds of theological students" and "embryo clergy"; worse, his views were bound to have a parlous effect upon "common folk," bewildering them with views which are meant to be the preserve of professional theologians and clerics. I will quote Mozley again:

CHAPTER EIGHT: ERSKINE AND F.D. MAURICE

> We enter on such a question [as the meaning of aionios] with great reluctance, but as one already brought into *public* discussion, and obtruded upon the attention of the *whole world* [so] we cannot avoid noticing it, though we see, as clearly as any one the evil of bringing so deep and mysterious a doctrine *into the common field*, and subjecting it to *ordinary criticism*, and cannot therefore but express our deep regret that Mr. Maurice should have thought it necessary to bring it forward and excite a controversy about it.[22]

More operative than this explicit clericalism, however, was the fear that Maurice's universalism would lead inevitably to antinomianism. Would not such views as Maurice taught overthrow the powerful sanctions of religion which are rightly contained within the doctrine of eternal punishment? And are not such sanctions legitimate stimulants and motives for moral living? Does not the creed of universalism lead to ethical chaos and to a radical diminution of the reality of sin? To such questions James Rigg (who was to Maurice very much what Andrew Thomson was to Erskine) responded with firm and unassailable conviction. A God who is a loving Father but not also a stern judge, Rigg believed, is not the God revealed in Scripture. If there is no retribution, no punishment, if there is no day of reckoning, then Christianity will surely evolve into a vapid religion, robbed of its strength and devoid of purpose. "Many a one," wrote Rigg, "who dies in the Lord will primarily have owed his salvation to a fear of the divine sanctions of religion which God's power and grace have impressed upon his mind. The fear of hell has, by God's grace, turned him from sin and opened his eyes to the joys of heaven."[23] Accordingly, Rigg warned that if Maurice's views on eternal punishment were not condemned then we can expect a "fearful increase of reckless wickedness." He spelled this out in gloomy detail:

> If [Maurice's doctrine is true], not only the peasant and the beggar, but the cold-blooded murderer, the brutal ravisher, the most fiendish of slave-drivers, all the children of the devil on earth, and all the demons of hell, may rejoice and sing merry songs together.[24]

It seems clear, then, that more than biblical or doctrinal orthodoxy was at stake, although the rhetoric employed by Maurice's detractors often disguised this fact. Appeals to orthodoxy or to the "Gospel" were iterated with sustained determination, but such appeals did not always address the heart of the matter. Rigg, for instance, was quite insistent that "Mr. Maurice is never and nowhere the preacher of a Gospel of salvation to a guilty and fallen race, through faith in the atoning merits of Christ's blood."[25] Rigg, of course, was quite right; such a view, based as it is on the Fall as its starting point, was totally antithetical to Maurice's understanding of the Gospel. Again, Rigg complained that "[n]ever does [Maurice] preach to a sinful world of a future punishment or exhort man to 'flee from the wrath to come.' Whatever else he may preach, he does *not* preach Christ's

Gospel."[26] Here, too, Rigg was quite right, since for Maurice, as for Erskine, a Gospel based on fear is not Good News, and the oft-repeated reference to the phrase from Luke 3:7 ("... flee from the wrath to come") was hardly a text to which Maurice drew attention. It was, however, a key scriptural text for his critics. Robert Candlish is a case in point. He composed a 483-page rejoinder to the *Theological Essays*, attacking Maurice's universalism in much the same vein as did Rigg, concluding his argument with this pious observation:

> I thank God continually that it is in preaching the gospel of the kingdom I am called to speak of the wrath to come; but woe unto me if I leave any to whom I reach under the impression that they may cast away from them the fear of suffering, and that for endless ages, the vengeance of eternal fire.[27]

Maurice was, of course, not without his friends and supporters. Erskine spoke for many of them when he wrote in November of 1853:

> Have you observed in the papers that the Council of King's College have deposed Maurice on account of heretical doctrines, taught in that volume [*Theological Essays*] which I gave you? I understand that the point is the denial of the unending duration of the future punishment. I congratulate him on being a martyr in such a cause; but I should be sorry if at this day the Church of England, as a body, confirms such a sentence. If spiritual perfection consists (as they would all admit it does) in the love of God, of men, and of all righteousness, it is not easy to see how such a doctrine as the eternity of punishment can lead to it. Men cannot be frightened into love; and they cannot easily realise God as a God of love, if such a doctrine be believed. (Hanna, p. 302)

Later Erskine was to write in a letter to Julia Wedgwood that Maurice was a man "prepared to carry out all his convictions without any cowardly hesitations" (Hanna, p. 381). And to Maurice himself (upon receiving a a copy of *The Doctrine of Sacrifice*), Erskine wrote that "[i]f the rash of censures which have been passed upon your Essays have led to this production, good has certainly come out of evil; and if your censurer himself reads these discourses, I cannot but think that his heart must smite him for what he has said" (Hanna, p. 310).[28]

One of the most touching tributes paid to Maurice at the time of his deposition came from the pen of Alfred, Lord Tennyson (Maurice was Godfather to Tennyson's son). The first few lines of his poem, entitled "To the Rev. F.D. Maurice," read as follows:

> Come, when no graver cares employ,

CHAPTER EIGHT: ERSKINE AND F.D. MAURICE

Godfather, come and see your boy;
Your presence will be sun in winter,
Making the little one leap for joy.

For, being of that honest few
Who give the Fiend himself his due,
Should eighty-thousand college councils
Thunder 'Anathema,' friend, at you,

Should all our churchmen foam in spite
at you, so careful of the right,
Yet one lay-hearth would give you welcome —
Take it and come — to the Isle of Wight.[29]

Although it does not appear that Thomas Erskine and John Frederick Denison Maurice saw each other with any great frequency, their letters to each other give ample evidence that there grew between them an intimate bond of friendship; their respect for each other was as genuine as it was steadfast. As late as 1867 (three years before Erskine died), Maurice wrote to his friend as follows:

> Our good friend the Bishop of Argyll [Alexander Ewing] has written to me to say how much he should like to tell my congregation [St. Peter's, Vere Street] some of the truth which he has learnt from God's Spirit through you, and I have written to say how much I should desire that he would and that I might be one of the congregation.[30]

It is not known whether such an event ever took place, but the image of Maurice sitting in the congregation listening to Ewing speak of the person to whom both he and Maurice were so deeply indebted is a delightful one.

And just a few months later (January, 1868), after a visit with Erskine, Maurice wrote in a similar vein:

> I do indeed look back with much wonder and thankfulness to the intercourse with you which inaugurated the beginning of the year for me. There is so much in the interchange of convictions even if one receives nothing fresh; but you gave me what was a quickening and renewal of thought and life, that had been in me doubtless, but that were not clearly or consciously in me, so that I felt you to be truly an instrument of the Spirit doing and fulfilling His work.[31]

Apart from the testimony of Maurice himself, not a few students of his theology have commented upon the impression made upon his thought by Erskine. Olive Brose, for instance, put it very simply: Erskine, she wrote, "led [Maurice] to see that the arbitrary Despot-God of popular orthodoxy was a perversion of that One whose character was altogether righteous."[32] Florence Higham's observation is also worthy of note: "Erskine ... helped Maurice so much because [he] combined the personal approach to Christ with a fervent repudiation of all that was exclusive in Calvinism."[33] It must also be said that Erskine was equally appreciative of Maurice's many contributions to his own theology: the influence was mutual. Comments such as "I always find instruction in your thoughts" (Hanna, p. 476) appear frequently in his letters to Maurice. Further, although Maurice was considerably more profound a theologian than Erskine (his writings address a seemingly infinite variety of topics[34]), whereas Erskine was by comparison a theological "amateur,"[35] they shared to a remarkable degree many views in common. Three are worth mentioning, if only briefly.

(1) In Chapter II of his *The Brazen Serpent* (entitled "Christ the Head"), Erskine asserted time and again that Christ, rather than being a substitute for humanity, is the "representative" or "Head" of the human race. Or, as he wrote earlier, only if Christ died and rose as the "Head of the human family" do we have "any hope for eternity" (Evidence, p. 70). And, in his late 60s Erskine reiterated this theme:

> I believe that as Christ is the ground of man's being, and is actually in every man as the supplier of spiritual life, so He is also the Head of man, of the whole race of man, acting for the race ... as their Head and root; doing things not instead of them but for them, as a root does things for the branches. (Hanna, p. 393)

So, too, with F.D. Maurice. As Bernard Reardon has pointed out, Maurice was "especially impressed by Erskine's conception of humanity redeemed and renewed in Christ as its head, and his concomitant refusal to press the dire consequences of Adam's fall as the proper basis of a theology."[36] Alec Vidler, in his study of Maurice, chose to devote an entire chapter to this key concept, entitling it "The Head and King of our Race."[37] Both he and Torben Christensen saw fit to quote a significant passage from a letter Maurice wrote to J.M. Ludlow in 1853:

> I hope ... by God's grace that no fear of offending my best and dearest friends will keep me from proclaiming that truth of Christ as the actual Head of Man, which I was sent into the world to proclaim ...[38]

As with Erskine, then, so with Maurice; either of them could have written the following: "You are not looked upon as a sinful race; you are looked upon as a race of which Christ is the Head."[39] And for both Erskine and Maurice, it is clear that their assertion as to Christ being the Head of the human race was both an implication of, and a distinct contribution towards, their shared insistence as to the universality of salvation. It is not surprising, therefore, that their understanding of baptism was in many respects similar, although Erskine wrote very little on the subject (the church's "sacraments" were not a topic to which he gave much attention); Maurice, on the other hand, wrote extensively on the subject.

(2) It seems that neither Maurice nor Erskine believed baptism to be strictly or exclusively necessary to salvation. Baptism, that is, does not *make* one a child of God and an inheritor of the Kingdom. Rather, it is a declaration of something that is *already* true, namely, that we *are* the children of God and partakers of eternal life ("This *is* eternal life, to know God the Father and Jesus Christ whom He sent."). In no way, wrote Erskine, can we be made or make ourselves the sons and daughters of God since our faith requires that "we are already the sons [and daughters]" (Sp. Order, p. 121). Bishop Ewing may be called upon to reflect Erskine's views (as so often he did) in his observation that "[w]e are not the children of God because we are baptised, we are baptised because we are his children."[40] Erskine himself, in writing to Ewing, spoke of one's relation to Christ as being created in him: "I don't make this relation by my faith, or baptism, or anything else" (Ewing, VI.42).

It is well known that much of what Maurice wrote on baptism was directed against the views of Edward Bouverie Pusey, Regius Professor of Hebrew at Oxford and leading Tractarian. Pusey's concept, as Vidler has summarized it, "made out that baptism was an instantaneous event which took man out of his relation to Adam and made him a member of Christ."[41] But this was not all. To Maurice, Pusey's position was a mockery and he wrote of the "misery" that Pusey's Tract on Baptism caused him. If Pusey's doctrine is true, he claimed, then

> the baptised child was holy for a moment after its baptism [but] in committing [post-baptismal] sin it had lost its purity. That could only be recovered by acts of repentance and a system of ascetical discipline.[42]

Michael Ramsey has suggested that the difference between Maurice and Pusey was that the latter believed that the former denied that anything *happened* in baptism (reducing the rite to a mere public affirmation that the child was already a child of God) while the former accused the latter of postulating a change in the divine favor produced by the ritual itself.[43] The controversy between the two was long and bitter, with each starting from assumptions and coming to conclusions that were entirely antithetical to each other.

Pusey's view struck Maurice as mechanical and transactional. The horror of it, thought Maurice, was that it was directly wedded to Pusey's insistence on the "biblical" and "orthodox" doctrine of everlasting punishment. Erskine and Maurice's more liberal view, however, again, was a direct implication of, and a contributing factor to, their shared assertion as to the universality of salvation.

(3) A third area of agreement between Erskine and Maurice had to do with their response to the advent of biblical criticism, especially as represented by the publication in 1860 of *Essays and Reviews* and by the writings of John William Colenso, Bishop of Natal. We have already seen that for Erskine biblical criticism posed no ultimate threat: "I am prepared to hear any criticism of the book, they do not trouble me in the least." What did trouble him, however, was that for many people whose faith was founded on the inerrancy of scripture, any criticism of the biblical narratives which suggested that they were not literally true could very well be destructive of their faith. This was Erskine's major concern. To a certain extent Maurice agreed: "I feel as Mr. Erskine does," he wrote to Ewing, "how hopeless it is to extract any theology or humanity from the 'Essays and Reviews'."[44] At the same time he was "greatly distressed" by the attacks made by the church establishment on the authors of that volume (who were ridiculed as Septem contra Christum). Too often, he felt, the defensive and offensive appeals to a rigid orthodoxy were but a disguise that covers one's atheism,[45] so he did not himself join the chorus of angry attackers. As Ieuan Ellis has put it, apart from his *The Mote and the Beam*[46] in which he articulated "his reservations and qualifications about both the essayists and their opponents," Maurice refused to join in the "agitation" caused by *Essays and Reviews*.[47] In the long run, however, Maurice believed as Erskine did, namely, that "[y]ou cannot produce faith or understanding by criticism. You cannot shake faith or understanding by criticism."[48]

In respect to Colenso, however, it was another matter altogether. In an undated letter to Colenso, the tone of which was gracefully irenic, Erskine wrote:

> I feel that I shrink from what you have done, and yet I can conceive your acting perfectly conscientiously. When I think of your criticisms I often seem to hear the voice of the Great Teacher saying, "I have many things to say unto you, but you cannot bear them now," as a call to thoughtful tenderness for our brethren. (Hanna, p. 400)[49]

Maurice was less irenic; the relationship between him and the Bishop of Natal was guarded at best, acerbic at worst. In a letter to a friend, Maurice suggested that Colenso should in fact resign his bishopric. And when the two of them did in fact meet, Colenso averred that anyone holding Maurice's views should resign his living.[50] Neither did in fact resign (although Maurice, as a somewhat staged gesture, threatened to do so). Unhappily, though, "[Maurice] and Colenso remained estranged."[51]

Both Erskine and Maurice were "pre-critical" in their understanding of the Bible and of biblical authority. They must have been taken somewhat by surprise by the advent of biblical criticism. Neither subscribed to the doctrine of verbal

CHAPTER EIGHT: ERSKINE AND F.D. MAURICE

inspiration or textual inerrancy (although Erskine, as we have seen, came close to doing so early on), but neither was comfortable with the implications of Benjamin Jewett's article in *Essays and Reviews* or with Colenso's studies of the Pentateuch. While Erskine's response was by and large pastoral, with a concern for "simple believers," Maurice's was more academic. Their faith, however, as well as their confidence in the abiding significance of Scripture, remained as strong as ever.

Although the writings of both Thomas Erskine and F.D. Maurice gave rise to acrimonious controversy (largely because of their universalism), neither was at heart a controversialist. As they shared a deep distrust of rigid theological systems,[52] so too they were united in their distrust of the sectarian spirit. Each would have subscribed to the Coleridgian dictum that if one loves Christianity more than truth, then one will come to love sect more than Christianity, and finally come to love self best of all.

If, as I have intimated, Erskine was a very private person, Maurice was considerably more active in the public realm; yet each was a man of deep humility. I am convinced that it was out of this humility that the near greatness of Thomas Erskine and the proven greatness of F.D. Maurice grew. The controversies that swirled around them in no way detracted from the influence that their theology has had upon subsequent generations. Maurice is read and studied extensively today. Erskine's influence, while less well known, deserves to be recognized as well and respected for its liveliness, its faithfulness, and its sustained engagement with the well-springs of Christianity, a Christianity that rejoices in the character of God.

Writing in 1877, seven years after Erskine's death and five years after Maurice's, an anonymous reviewer of the first volume of Hanna's *The Letters of Thomas Erskine*, in a passage part of which I quoted earlier, wrote (with perhaps pardonable hyperbole) that

> [i]t is now more than half a century since Thomas Erskine ... published the first of those Essays which, as we believe, are revolutionizing the whole theology of the North; and not of the North only, for no less a profound thinker than Frederick Maurice has expressly informed us that it was this lay theologian — a second St. Stephen in this respect — who first brought home to his mind the conviction that we have a Gospel for the whole world, and not merely for a few picked favourites here and there. Mr. Erskine, indeed, inaugurated a method of inquiry which is more radically affecting theological thought than even the Theses of Luther himself. Luther's quarrel with Rome was one of *degree* ... Erskine's [with the reigning orthodoxy of his day] was one of *kind*.[53]

Notes to Chapter Eight

1. Frank Mauldin McClain, *Maurice: Man and Moralist* (London, SPCK, 1972), p. 3. See C.R. Sanders, *Coleridge and the Broad Church Movement* (Durham, NC: Duke University Press, 1942), p. 184.
2. Alec R. Vidler, *F.D. Maurice and Company* (London: SCM, 1966), p. 242. See also Olive J. Brose, *Frederick Denison Maurice: Rebellious Conformist* (Athens, OH: University of Ohio Press, 1971), pp. 47-49.
3. In addition to the epistle dedicatory to Erskine in his *Prophets and Kings of the Old Testament*, see also Maurice's letter to Derwent Coleridge in the second edition of his *The Kingdom of Christ*.
4. Unfortunately, about Lucy we know nothing else, not even her last name. Frank McClain once observed to me in conversation that he likes to think of her as Saint Lucy!
5. Frederick Maurice (ed.), *The Life of Frederick Denison Maurice* (New York: Scribner's, 1884), Vol. I, p. 43.
6. *Ibid.*
7. Florence Higham has written that Lucy "told [Maurice] to read Erskine, and so he found a sheet anchor to which to cling, until he knew where he stood in matters of doctrine," but I can find no reference to support this statement. *Frederick Denison Maurice* (London: SCM, 1947), p. 18.
8. Maurice, *Life*, Vol. I, p. 108.
9. *Ibid.*, p. 21. Maurice also wrote appreciatively, in the same letter, of Erskine's pastoral activity: "I hear from those who know him that ... if he hears of a friend or a distant acquaintance or a stranger and an enemy within a reasonable distance of 500 or 600 miles [!] who is in distress and would be the better for his counsel, he starts off and spends as much time as they will let him, with them."
10. Maurice, *Life*, Vol. I, p. 183.
11. Later (1841), Erskine was to write of Maurice in gentler terms. In recommending Maurice's *The Kingdom of Christ* to a friend he noted: "The writer is a friend of mine, whom I value highly as a man of great worth and of great intellectual power" (Hanna, p. 255). Geoffrey Rowell believes that Erskine and Maurice first met in 1833, but I have been unable to find substantiation for this dating. *Hell and the Victorians*, p. 73.
12. Maurice, *Life*, Vol. II, p. 150; also in Hanna, pp. 101f.
13. F.D. Maurice, *The Prophets and Kings of the Old Testament* (Cambridge: Macmillan, 1853), pp. vii, ix-x. The dedication is dated 11 November 1882.
14. F.D. Maurice, *Theological Essays* (New York: Harper, 1957), p. 323. The most succinct articulation of Maurice's universalism is to be found in his letter to F.J.A. Hort of 23 November 1849, some years before the publication of *Theological Essays*. See Maurice, *Life*, Vol. II, pp. 15-23.
15. *Ibid.*
16. *Ibid.*, p. 317.

CHAPTER EIGHT: ERSKINE AND F.D. MAURICE

17 *Ibid.*, p. 314.

18 F.D. Maurice, *The Word 'Eternal,' and the Punishment of the Wicked: A Letter to the Rev. Dr. Jelf* (from the second edition, New York: C.S. Francis, 1854), p. 6. It was Dr. Blomfield, then Bishop of London, who first called Maurice's "errors" to Dr. Jelf's attention. Ironically, Dr. Jelf, Maurice's major opponent on the Council, held the position of Principal, a post which Maurice himself had been offered earlier but had turned down. It is also interesting to note that Maurice, in a letter to Charles Kingsley (19 July 1853) wrote: "I knew when I wrote the sentences about eternal death that I was writing my own sentence at King's College." *Life*, Vol. II, p. 168.

19 London: J.H. Parker, 1854. Maurice referred to his controversy with Mansel as "my difference with those who think that revelation does not reveal." So Arthur Rogers, *Men and Movements in the English Church* (New York, 1898), p. 301.

20 R.H. Hutton, *Aspects of Religious and Scientific Thought* (London: Macmillan, 1899), p. 269.

21 J.B. Mozley, *Essays Historical and Theological* (London, 1892 [third edition]), Vol. 2, p. 272. The essay on Maurice appeared originally in *The Christian Remembrancer* of January 1854.

22 Mozley, *op. cit.*, Vol. 2, p. 281.

23 James H. Rigg, *Modern Anglican Theology* (second edition; London, 1859), p. 195.

24 *Ibid.*, p. 196. Compare this with the similar sentiment of David Davidson quoted above, Chapter Two, at note 29.

25 Rigg, p. 121.

26 *Ibid.*, pp. 121f.

27 Robert S. Candlish, *Examination of Mr. Maurice's Theological Essays* (London: Nisbet, 1854), p. 471.

28 That Erskine did not agree with all that Maurice wrote in *The Doctrine of Sacrifice* is suggested by a letter to his sister, Mrs. James Paterson, dated 14 February 1855 (Hanna, p. 310), and by his letter to Bishop Ewing of February, 1861 (Hanna, pp. 408f.).

29 Tennyson's poem is dated January, 1854.

30 Maurice, *Life*, Vol. II, p. 562.

31 *Ibid.*, p. 572.

32 Olive J. Brose, *op. cit.*, p. 72.

33 Florence Higham, *op. cit.*, p. 123.

34 See the extensive bibliography in Frank McClain, *op. cit.* pp. 177-196.

35 The term "amateur" was used by D.J. Vaughan, "Scottish Influence upon English Theological Thought," *Contemporary Review*, Vol. 32 (1878), p. 471.

36 B.M.G. Reardon, *From Coleridge to Gore* (London: Longman, 1971), p. 398.

37 Alec Vidler, *op. cit.*, pp. 38-61.

38 Maurice, *Life*, Vol. II, p. 161. See also Torben Christensen, *The Divine Order: A Study in F.D. Maurice's Theology* (Leiden: Brill, 1973), p. 73.

[39] F.D. Maurice, *The Epistles of St. John* (London 1881), p. 110.
[40] Alexander Ewing, *Address*, p. 74.
[41] Vidler, *op. cit.*, p. 97.
[42] Maurice, *Life*, Vol. I, p. 237. For an extended discussion of baptism see Ch. 4 of Maurice's *The Kingdom of Christ*, Vol. 1 (new edition; London: SCM), pp. 258-288. And for Erskine's view of "Puseyism" see Hanna, pp. 386-391.
[43] Arthur Michael Ramsey, *F.D. Maurice and the Conflicts of Modern Theology* (Cambridge: Cambridge University Press, 1951), p. 35.
[44] Maurice, *Life*, Vol. II, p. 384.
[45] *Ibid.*, p. 383.
[46] F.D. Maurice, *The Mote and the Beam: A Clergyman's Lessons from the Present Panic*, No. II of *Tracts for Priests and People* (London, 1861).
[47] Ieuan Ellis, *Seven Against Christ: A Study of 'Essays and Reviews'* (Leiden: Brill, 1980), p. 131.
[48] F.D. Maurice, *The Claims of the Bible and of Science* (London: Macmillan, 1863), pp. 35-36; quoted by Olive Brose, *op. cit.*, p. 271.
[49] See also Erskine's letter to Maurice of 11 October 1862 (Hanna, pp. 341-342).
[50] Maurice, *Life*, Vol. II, p. 422.
[51] So Olive Brose, *op. cit.*, p. 270. She goes on to say that Maurice was one of those few who "escaped the crudities of either verbal inspiration or destructive criticism."
[52] "The freer one is from Church system in this country," wrote Maurice, "the freer one is able to serve the Church." *Life*, Vol. I, p. 415. Out of his deep concern for church unity, Maurice refused to join any party (Liberal, Evangelical, &c.) but was aware that someone might install him as the leader of the "No Party" party! See *Life*, Vol. I, p. 239.
[53] *The Spectator*, 23 June 1877, pp. 793-794.

APPENDIX

It has already been noted in the Preface that Erskine's works are today "almost unattainable." For this reason the following excerpts from his writings are here included. They have been chosen so as to give examples of the peculiarities of Erskine's rhetorical style and of his use of scripture. Too, they have been selected in order to give more extended documentation concerning some of the major theological issues which Erskine addressed in the course of his lifetime.

To Madame De Staël. 4 September 1829.

Gaussen is quite right in telling you that I do not forget you before God. But I am much ashamed of my negligence as a correspondent, especially when I consider what God has given me to correspond about. My dear friend, we may speak to each other of God's love — God's forgiving love in giving us His Son to be the propitiation for our sins. He has given His Son to you and to me, and in Him He has given us all things. When the bible says, "Acquaint thyself with God and be at peace" [Job 21:22], it means to say that there is something in God which necessarily gives peace to everyone that knows it. If a soul is not at peace, the only reason is because it does not know God. If Joseph's brethren, as they stood before him, and not knowing who he was, but hearing him speak roughly to them, had been told, "This is your brother Joseph," they would immediately have been filled with terror, thinking that he would now take vengeance on them for their treatment of him; but if they could have looked into his heart, and had seen there a forgiving love which yearned over them, and which was not in the smallest degree affected by their unkindness to him, it is evident that although they would have reproached themselves far more than they had ever done before, yet they would have had a perfect deliverance from all personal fears on their own account, they would have seen a ground of confidence in their brother's character which must at once have given them peace. If Joseph had loved all of them except one, then it could not have been said to that one, "Acquaint thyself with Joseph and be at peace," for the knowledge that he was really excluded from Joseph's love would have given him terror and not peace. So if there were a single being whom God did not love, then it could not have been said to that being, "Acquaint thyself with God and be at peace." But as it is said generally to all, it must also be true to all that God loves them, and that it is only necessary for them to know God's feelings towards them, and to look into God's heart, in order to have perfect peace. This is the meaning of being saved by faith. If God did not love, and had not forgiven us, our salvation could only be produced by our doing something that might make a change in God's feelings towards us; that would be salvation by works, or by our doing something. But since God does love us and has forgiven us, we need not do anything to change God's feelings, and all that is necessary for our peace and confidence is to know what the actual state of God's feelings are towards us, and this is salvation by faith, *c'est à dire*, salvation by knowing our real circumstances. All human religions are founded on the principle that man must do something or feel something, or believe something, in order to make God love him and forgive him; whereas God's religion just contains a declaration that nothing of the kind is necessary on our part in order to make God forgive us, for that he hath, *déjà*, already, loved us and forgiven us, and given us His Son, and in Him all things. He hath declared this to the whole race without any exception, as a truth to each individual; so that the difference between the most miserable hater of God and the happiest child of God does not consist in this, that God loves the one and does not love the other; but in this, that the one knows God's love to himself and the other does not. It is the same difference as there is between two men standing with their faces to the sun, the one with his eyes shut and the other with his eyes open ...

And why has God taken such pains to satisfy us that He has indeed loved and forgiven all men? Just in order that every individual might see in God a perfect ground for confidence. Unless you know that God has forgiven you, and that He loves you, you cannot have any confidence in Him; and unless you have full confidence in Him, you cannot have peace with Him, you cannot open your heart to Him, you cannot love Him. It is the belief of His forgiving love to yourself which alone can open your heart to Him. This is the true meaning of the doctrine of personal assurance. It is not that God saves a man because he has an assurance of his own personal salvation, but that our hearts cannot open to God until we are satisfied that He loves ourselves with a forgiving love. Until we are satisfied of His love to us, we cannot love Him; and therefore we cannot obey Him, for there is no obedience without love. This is the meaning of John vi. 28, 29. When the multitude that were following Jesus asked Him, What shall we do that we may work the works of God? He answered them, "This is the work of God, that ye believe on Him whom He hath sent." Their question was, "How are we to obey the commandments of God?" and his answer was, "You must begin by believing in God's forgiving love to you in sending His Son to be the propitiation for your sins." For until you believe this, it is impossible for you to obey the least of God's commandments, because the least of His commandments requires love, and you cannot love Him until you are assured that He loves you. The knowledge of our own personal forgiveness and of our being personally embraced in the love of God is the first step in Christianity. No one is a Christian until he knows this. And how may every one know this? See John i.29, 2 Cor. v.19, 1 Tim. ii.1-6, 1 John ii.2. The personal assurance rises out of the general declaration of forgiveness to all, and peace and joy and love rise out of the personal assurance.

I long much to see both Madame de Broglie and yourself, but it seems to me that God has called me to be a witness for truth at home. I am continually engaged in preaching to small congregations at present — three hours every day, and often much more. If God lets me see it to be my duty to cross the Channel this autumn to see you, it will be a great delight to me. Give my most brotherly love in Christ Jesus to Madame de Broglie and to your dear mother. Give your child a kiss and a blessing from me, as from one who loved his father. Talk over this letter with Madame de B., and let me know how you feel about it.

(Hanna, pp. 116-119)

ON LOVE

We can only have love in us by knowing that God hath loved us first, and yet this love is not gratitude, and of course not selfish. The knowledge that God has loved us and forgiven us is necessary to our having confidence in God, and so opening our hearts to let God in. But this knowledge does not produce the love, it only opens the door of the heart to let it in; God is himself the love. And when he enters us, we shall love him with himself, with his own love, just as we see the sun with its own light, that is, with himself. We love God because he first loved us; as we see the sun because he first shone on us. There is no other light by which we can see the sun but his own light, and there is no other love by which we can love God but his own love. There is no other love; everything else which takes the name of love is a spurious thing. "Love is of God," and he who has not God dwelling in him cannot love truly; he has no love wherewith to love; and therefore, when we are commanded to love, we are in fact commanded to receive God into us. We are not called to love our fellow creatures *because* God loves them, but *as* God loves them, with the very same love, that is, with God in us loving them. God's love is entirely and essentially different from anything which goes by the name of love in the creature, just as different as God is different from the creature. And therefore we mistake the matter altogether when we confound God's love in the heart with the gratitude and affection produced by the kindness of our fellow-creatures to us.

God's love cannot be separated from himself, and so it is written, "he that dwelleth in love dwelleth in God and God in him" [1 John 4:16]. A man's having real love in him can be accounted for only in one way; he must have God dwelling in him; he could not have love otherwise, for there is no other love; and so the love of God in the creature is not a mere readiness to do the will of God *when known*, as the love of an earthly parent is just such a readiness; the love of God is *knowledge* of his will and *conformity* to it, as well as readiness to do it; the love of God is actually the fulfilling of the law because *it is God himself who is the law, dwelling in the creature*. Love is the blessing of the new covenant, "I will put my law in their hearts" [Jeremiah 31:33 & cf. Hebrews 13:7], and not a mere readiness to do it. This is the meaning of the dispensation of the Spirit. The Spirit is love. And so, when it is written that "love believeth all things" [1 Cor. 13:7], it is not meant that there is a facility or proneness in love to believe or hope anything; but the meaning is that love, which is God's own Spirit in the creature, stands in God's counsel and knows his mind, and therefore recognises all his revelations, and hopes or desires all that he purposes; the meaning is the same when it is said, "The Spirit searcheth all things, even the deep things of God" [1 Cor. 2:10]. Man's love flatters its objects; man's love suffers sin in its objects; man's love comes forth on those who have qualities fitted to attract it; it comes forth on those who are agreeable to him, on those who are estimable in his eyes, on those who flatter his selfish feelings in some way or other. God's love is the opposite of all this. He loves, not because any object attracts his love, but because he is love. "He commendeth his love to us, in that whilst we were sinners, Christ died for us" [Romans 5:8]. This greatest proof of his love is the very thing which declares his unutterable abhorrence of the characters of those whom he thus loved. His love spares not the feelings of its objects; it is a consuming fire; the cross declares the love; this love crucifies those whom it loves, because "it rejoiceth not in iniquity, but rejoiceth in the truth" [1 Cor. 13:6]; "it loveth righteousness and hateth iniquity." It is love that hateth iniquity; nothing else can hate it. Love is the fulfilling of the law, and one part of the law is, Thou shalt not suffer sin in thy brother. Love is the fulfilling of the law, and what is holiness but a conformity to the law? So love is holiness and holiness is love. Love is that fire of which it is written, "Who among us shall dwell with the devouring fire?" [*ibid.*, 15], he and only he can dwell with this love. Love is a state and may exist without any object, and so it is said, "*He that loveth* is born of God" [1 John 4:7]. *"He that loveth,"* without even supposing an object. Loving what? Just loving. The man is supposed to be living in a state of love. And so enmity is a state, it is a condition of the natural man. Let no one say, that if another meaning is to be attached to the word *love* in the Bible, than its ordinary meaning amongst men, then the whole Bible becomes unintelligible to us, and speaks to us in an unknown tongue; for the truth is, that the whole Bible is written just to explain this matter to us, just to show us what love is, and to show us how entirely different it is from what man calls love. Love is the birth from above, the everlasting life, and enmity is the natural and universal condition of fallen man, until born of the Spirit. Love is the Spirit. "God so *loved* the world as to give his Son" [cf. John 3:16], and he that believes this love receives it into him, he receives the Spirit, he is born of the Spirit, he hath everlasting life. Love is the bruiser of the serpent. The serpent was a murderer from the beginning [cf. John 8:44]; love alone can bruise his head. And love is of God alone. Love is the name of God, and for that name's sake Jesus was hated by men, "For my love, they are my adversaries" [Psalm 109:4], and in that name it was that Jesus overcame, "They came about me like bees, but in the *name* of the Lord will I destroy them" [Psalm 118:11-12]. And it is for this name's sake also that his disciples are to be hated of all men, as it is in this name they are to set up their banner.

We are living and moving and having our being [cf. Acts 17:28] in this love, in the midst of it. We are surrounded and embraced and pressed upon by it, and it is a grieved and grieving love, it is the very love which wept and groaned and agonised in Jesus. The sufferings of Jesus were not a manifestation of a passing temporary thing; they were the manifestations of the mind of the unchangeable God towards sinful man. Reader, this is a mighty and an awful reality; we are living enclosed in the substance of a loving omnipotent God, whose Spirit is continually grieved by the madly wicked resistance that we make to be dwelt in by him, and so to be made partakers of his nature, of his sorrow, of his joy.

(*The Brazen Serpent*, pp. 283-287)

To Louis Gaussen. 7 December 1832.

Although I have had much enjoyment in meeting you once more in this world, yet I have also suffered much, chiefly because I am sensible that in witnessing for God's truth to you, I often sinned against the law of love and meekness and patience. May the Lord forgive the sin, and mercifully overrule, so that it may not act in your mind as a reason against any truth which you heard from me. May the good Lord give you the spirit of a little child in waiting upon Him for light on those things which were the subjects of our conversation. My dear brother, it appears to me clear from Scripture that the blessing which God holds out to man through the work of redemption is a *real and substantial restoration* to the image of God, which is to be effected by man becoming the habitation of God through the Spirit (Eph. iv.24, ii.22, and 2 Cor. vi.16). This is not a fictitious righteousness, for then it would be also a fictitious blessedness, but it is a real conformity to the will of God. *This* is the mercy which God promised from the beginning, "that He would grant unto us that we, being delivered from the hand of our enemies, *might serve Him without fear in holiness and righteousness before Him* all the days of our life" (Luke 1.72-75). See to the same purpose, Acts iii.26; and amongst innumerable passages in the Old Testament let me specially direct your attention to Jeremiah xxxi.33, and to Ezekiel xxxvi.25, 26, which most strikingly declare this truth. And there is but one kind of true righteousness, namely, the character of God, for "none is good save one, that is, God" (Luke xviii.19), and therefore, in order that a man should be righteous or good, he must have God dwelling in him; and thus Paul writes, "that the righteousness of the law is fulfilled only in those who walk not after the flesh but after the Spirit," which is God dwelling in man (Rom. viii.4). That the righteousness which God desires to see in us is a real substantial thing is manifest also from those passages which speak of the judgment to come; thus Rom. ii.6, 2 Cor. v.10; read also to the same purpose 1 John ii.29, iii.7, 8, 9, 10. "Christ came not to destroy the law, but to fulfill" (Matt. v.17). It is quite manifest that there can be no true blessedness without this true righteousness, and that the fulfillment of that word, "Enter into the joy of thy Lord" (Matt. xxv.21), requires the fulfillment of those other words, "partakers of His holiness," and "partakers of the divine nature" (Heb. xii.10; 2 Peter i.4). And thus we are brought to that mighty thing which is the great object through all the Bible, namely, the mystery of godliness, the wonder of ungodly creatures becoming godly, the manifestation of God in the flesh, which is the true restoration of the image of God to man.

When man hears of such a perfect righteousness, instead of rejoicing in the tidings of it, he is quite cast down, How am I ever to arrive at it? Has not God said, "The carnal mind is enmity against God, and is not subject to the law of God, neither indeed can be" [Romans 8:7]? This fear and dejection arises from his ignorance of God's righteousness, for he thinks he has to build up this perfect character for himself before he is entitled to have any confidence in God; and as he feels his inability to come up to this high standard, he either endeavors to lower the standard of duty down to what he believes himself capable of, which is the antinomianism of the Sadducee, or else he substitutes a doctrine in its place, or rather the perversion of the doctrine of justification by faith, because he thinks it easier to believe something than to have the perfect righteousness in reality, which is the antinomianism of the Pharisee. The Sadducee supposes that he is to open the door of his Father's house, which has been shut against him, by doing certain moral duties; the Pharisee thinks to open it by certain religious opinions; whereas the blessed truth is, that God has himself opened the door by rending the veil of the flesh of Jesus, and now calls every sinner, not to the task of opening the door, but to the privilege of entering by the opened and blood-sprinkled door, and of looking to God as a Father indeed, and of being a member of his family, partaking of all the interests and prospects of the family, namely, the advancement of Christ's kingdom on earth, and the expectation of the coming glory. This is the right place for a man to be in, c'est à dire, in his Father's family, and occupied with his Father's interests; this is his right place, the place for which he was created and redeemed; this is his righteousness, and in him is fulfilled the word spoken in Luke i.74, 75, and in Acts iii.26. But how is this righteousness to be the foundation of his confidence? So far from it, that this righteousness can only be produced by a confidence already existing. Confidence is the root of everything good in man, it cannot be founded on anything in man, but must be founded on something out of man (*au dehors de l'homme*). And what is it then that man's confidence is to be founded on? God. God has revealed Himself as the foundation of the sinner's confidence, and now in Christ He invites and commands all the sinners of the earth to give Him their confidence, because He is worthy of their confidence, "having made Him who knew no sin to become sin for them, that they might become the righteousness of God in Him" (2. Cor. v.21). God is the blessedness of the creature, and the punishment of sin in the creature is to be shut out or cut off from God; and as the punishment is pronounced in these words, "DEPART, *ye cursed*" [Matthew 25:41], so forgiveness of sin is pronounced in the words, "RETURN unto me, for I have redeemed you" [Isaiah 44:22]. No creature which had sinned could have any right to come to God, or to enjoy God, or to trust in God, unless God had put away that condemnation of "Depart, ye cursed," which is due to every sinner, and had said, "Come unto me all ye that labour" [Matthew 11:28], etc.; but God is saying during this day of grace to all sinners, "Come unto me," thus assuring them that they may well put their confidence in Him, because He loves them, and confirming this to them by revealing to them the blood and resurrection of Jesus as the ground on which this invitation is addressed to all men. God laid on Jesus the iniquities of us all, Jesus died under this weight, and God raised Him from the dead, thus declaring sin condemned and punished and the sinner freed. On this ground it is that God says to every sinner, "Trust in God." Trust in Him as your Father, your guide, your guard, your everlasting rest. Take no step without Him. Take no joy without Him. Let Him be your hope, your only hope, not that by thus hoping in Him you are to make Him what he was not before, but that by knowing what He is to you, you may be blessed in Him. "God hath raised Jesus from the dead, and given him glory, *afin que* our faith and hope may be in God." Those who know what God meant when He raised Jesus from the dead have faith and hope in God, and those who are without faith and hope in God are those who do not know the mind of God declared in the resurrection of Jesus (1 Peter i.21). "It is eternal life to know God as revealed in Christ," because it is in knowing Him that we enjoy Him and become partakers of His nature (2 Peter i:4). Every man who knows God has eternal life in that knowledge, and every man who has not eternal life is without it, in consequence of his ignorance of God (Eph. iv.18). Now surely it would be a great dishonor to God to suppose that we change Him by our knowledge or ignorance; we must therefore acknowledge that the heart of God towards every man is such that, if the man knew it, he could not but rejoice in it; for how else could it be life to him to know God? What then is to make me rejoice in God? A sight of God's heart as loving me, a knowledge of God's good-will concerning me? And how am I to get this sight and this knowledge? Jesus Christ hath come forth from the bosom of the Father to show us the heart of God. "He by the grace of God tasted death for every man" (Heb. ii.9); and then he said, "He that hath seen me hath seen the Father" [John 15:9]. It was this that made Jesus "the light of the world." He declared the Father to the world, to the end that whosoever knoweth the Father through Him might live by that knowledge. He came to seek and save the lost, by declaring to them the Father's heart, and as soon as they know that heart they are glad, they rejoice in salvation; but whilst they continue ignorant of God's heart they continue to be without eternal life in them. He came to seek and save the lost. God raised Him from the dead and gave Him glory, that the lost might be saved by putting their faith and hope in God. These lost souls, that is, all men, are called to put their faith and hope in God; they are called to trust in God, not because they have faith, but because God has raised Christ from the dead. A poor sinner rising from the murder of his brother is desired and invited to trust in God, to see God's forgiveness in that word, "Come unto me," and to put his faith and hope in God, because he hath raised Jesus from the dead. "God is the Saviour of all men, specially of those who believe" (1 Tim. iv.10). God's heart is a heart of forgiving love before we believe, but we cannot enjoy God, which is full salvation, without knowing or believing what His heart is to us.

You seem to me to rest not on what God is, but rather on what God has said, as distinct from God. Before the coming of Christ men might have made a distinction between God and His word: but now such a distinction is Socinianism, for God hath declared that the Word is God. When it is not God Himself we meet and trust in His Word, we are breaking the second commandment. Faith has become to the intellectual Protestant churches what the idols of silver and gold were to the Jewish and Popish churches. Why is a poor sinner to trust in God? Is it because God is good, or because *he* has faith? Am I to trust in God because "God was in Christ reconciling the world unto Himself, not imputing unto them their trespasses" [2 Cor. 5:19], or because I am justified by faith? Read the 78th Psalm, marking specially verses 7, 22, 35. God was always "their Rock and Redeemer," but whilst they believed it not, they put away His salvation — (as the sun is always our light, but when we shut our eyes we are in darkness). He was always their loving, forgiving Father, even in His punishments; yet they were like famine in the far country, sent to bring back the prodigal to his father's house. Do you not believe that the heart of God does indeed grieve and yearn over every sinner that continues at a distance from Him? and is not that grief, the grief of love, which desires the holy blessedness of the sinner? Yes, it is the grief of love. God created man to be the image of God, and holiness and blessedness. And God did this, because God is love. And this purpose of God towards man hath not changed, but has followed every individual man through every moment of his life, desiring that he should yet be the image of God. And God hath revealed this purpose fully in Jesus Christ, who by the grace of God tasted death for every man, and was raised from the dead into glory, that every man might have confidence in God's purpose, and might yield himself unto God to have that purpose accomplished in him. This restoration of the image is salvation. Salvation is not forgiveness of sin; it is not the remission of a penalty; it is not a safety. No, it is the blessed and holy purpose of God's love accomplished in the poor fallen creature's restoration of the divine image. And as this could only be effected by God dwelling in man, so the work of Christ has been God's taking possession of a part of the fallen nature and uniting Himself to it, without separating it from the rest of the mass of the nature, and in that part working perfect righteousness, and so ordering it that this part of the nature so possessed by God should become the new root and head of man, from which the Holy Spirit, given to him without measure, might flow forth, seeking entrance into every part of the nature wherever it can find an open heart. And to this end is the news of God's love in this great work declared to men, that they hearing it may have confidence in Him who hath thus loved them, and so open their hearts to let in His Spirit. So we have no need now to go out of our nature to meet God, and to get the eternal life (which is God's life), for God is in our own flesh, and the eternal life is in our own flesh, and we have but to know this loving God, and the longings of His heart over us, and to give Him our confidence, in order to receive His Spirit into us.

And Christ's work of atonement was perfected by His death, not only testifying the love of God to every man to be a love which would die for every man, but also testifying that when God would restore man He would not restore that natural life in which man had sinned, He would not remove His condemnation from that life on which He had pronounced sentence of death, and that He could not look on man well pleased until man had consented to the righteousness of this sentence and had willingly given up that natural life which had rebelled against God. The man Christ Jesus did this, and thus manifested the express image of the

Father, and so He was raised to be the second Adam, the mediator between God and man, between the God-nature and the man-nature. It is upon this ground that every man is invited and demanded to delight in God, and to drink out of the fountain of life which is His love. Now cannot it be said with propriety that any creature is a condemned creature, whilst it is commanded as well as permitted to enjoy such a God as this and to drink out of such a fountain as this? Can any creature be said to be unforgiven for whose blessedness God is at this very moment working with a love passing knowledge? *O fortunati nimium, sua si bona norint*! Read the 107th Psalm. The only true condemnation consists in being shut out from that fountain to which we are all urged and entreated to come that we may drink abundantly.

And surely when persons can acknowledge that God has given Christ for men and to men, and yet refuse to acknowledge that the Spirit has been also given as widely, they forget that Christ is God, and that in Him not one person only of the Trinity, but the whole Trinity, was manifested. I feel that to separate between the work of Christ and the character of God is Socinianism. So also I feel that to suppose Christ given and not the Spirit is not less Socinianism. It is denying that the Word is God. Do you not believe that every man is in a very different condition now from what he would have been had Christ not come into the world? The word to every man, if Christ had not come, would have been, "Depart, thou cursed," and now, in consequence of Christ's coming, the word to every man is, "Come to the waters," "Come unto me, thou weary one, and I will give thee rest." My brother, if the condemnation consist in the word, "Depart," tell me what is contained in the word "Come." When Paul declared this change of address, was it too much to call it the forgiveness of sins? Acts xiii.38. Compare this verse and the following one with 1 Timothy iv.10. These two verses are a commentary on the two words in Timothy, "The Saviour of all men, especially of those who believe." No man could approach God through Christ, unless Christ had eternal life or the Holy Spirit for him, for no man can come to God except in the Holy Spirit; thus every man has eternal life in Christ, and he has also the natural life; the first of these is holy and sinless and without condemnation, and the man who walks in it is righteous; the second is sinful and under condemnation, and he who walks in it, whether he has been a believer or not, walks under a condemnation. God does not change His judgment, nor does He call evil good, nor does He call good evil. Abiding in the faith of Jesus is abiding in eternal life — leaving Him is falling under condemnation. Beloved brother, this is the concluding sentence: May the God of peace fill you with peace in believing, and make you to abound in the knowledge of the love of Jesus.

Read 2 Peter, 1st chapter. Farewell.

(Hanna, pp. 186-195)

To Edward Craig. 1864.

Your epistle on the "Final Salvation of All Men from Sin" had been put into my hands by a friend who knew that the principles contained in it are those with which I have long concurred and sympathised: and having read it, I cannot help reaching out to you a brotherly hand, and saying, God speed you!

The title of your pamphlet has been, I think, well chosen. It is not a deliverance from punishment, but a deliverance from sin, that you desire or expect. All punishment appointed by God, whether it be the natural result of sin, or any superadded chastisement, is intended by him "for our profit, that we may be partakers of his holiness"; so that a deliverance from punishment, instead of being a thing desired, would in fact be equivalent to the deliverance of a sick man from the necessary and wise prescription of a skilful physician. This is the revealed purpose of punishment, — a purpose agreeing with the character of God, and with the relation in which He stands to men. He is the "righteous Father" — "who willeth not the death of a sinner; but that all should come to repentance" [cf. 2 Peter 3:9]. Let us hold fast to the purpose of God in all punishment, and remember that as it is the purpose of Him who changeth not, but who is the same yesterday, to-day, and for ever [cf. Hebrews 13:8], it cannot be a purpose confined to any one stage of our being, but must extend over all stages, and the whole duration of our being. It is surely most unreasonable to suppose that God should change His manner of dealing with us as soon as we quit this world, and that if we have resisted up to that moment His gracious endeavors to teach us righteousness, He should at once abandon the purpose for which He created and redeemed us, and give us up to the everlasting bondage of sin. Do we not feel that such a supposition is too horrible — that it is most dishonouring to Him who said, "I will never leave thee, nor forsake thee" [Hebrews 13:5] and "The mountains shall depart, and the hills be removed, but my kindness shall not depart from thee, neither shall the covenant of my peace be removed, saith the Lord that hath mercy on thee" [Isaiah 54:10]?

This reasoning agrees with the argument presented to us in the 5th chapter of the Epistle to the Romans, where the Apostle, in setting forth the fulness of the redemption by Christ, declares that the benefit through Him is, in extent, parallel to the evil introduced by Adam; that is, that as the evil affects all without exception, so the blessedness embraces all without exception. Let any one read the 12th and 18th verses of that chapter, as if in juxtaposition, which they really are by construction, and he will find himself constrained to admit that this and nothing less could have been the meaning of the writer. Indeed, through the whole chapter there is a preponderating advantage thrown into the scale of the redemption, to the effect that not only were the evils of the fall met by the salvation of Christ, but that the gain far surpassed the loss, so that it is really contrary to sound criticism to hold that, in that most marked and most remarkable passage, where the comparative results of the fall and the restoration are expressly considered, any ground is allowed or given for a doubt as to the final salvation of the whole human race. The 11th chapter of the Epistle is pervaded by the same doctrine, being a declaration that God's election does not affect the truth and certainty of the final salvation of men, but relates to the temporary use which He makes of individuals or nations to accomplish the ends of His government. I know well that most people in this country feel that all such arguments and expositions are met and overturned by the solemn words of our Lord in the 25th chapter of St. Matthew, and by other passages of like import. I feel, on the contrary, that the passages I have quoted from the Epistle to the Romans ought really to be considered as the ruling passages on the question, and that those from St. Matthew, and others of the same class, should be explained by them, and in accordance with them, because in them the fall and restoration are expressly compared with each other, in their whole results, and the entire superiority claimed for the restoration in amount of benefit and entire equality in point of extent; all which would seem to me to be utterly nullified by the fact of a single human spirit being abandoned and consigned to a permanent state of sin and misery. I therefore understand that awful scene represented in St. Matthew as declaring the certainty of the connection between sin and misery, but not as a finality. I do not believe that *aionios*, the Greek word rendered "eternal" and "everlasting" by our translators, really has that meaning. I believe that it refers to man's essential or spiritual state, and not to time, either infinite or finite. Eternal life is living in the love of God; eternal death is living in self; so that a man may be in eternal life or in eternal death for ten minutes, as he changes from the one state to the other.

There is no lack of arguments for the general view which I have taken of this subject, drawn either from conscience or the Scriptures, or both. There is one that cannot but have great weight with all who fairly consider it. Throughout the Old Testament, God is more constantly presented to us as a Father than in any other character; and in the New, our Lord speaks of it as the chief purpose of His appearance in this world, to reveal His Father as the Father of the whole human race. In both, frequent appeals are made to our sense of the love and desires and obligations of an earthly parent towards his children, in order to impress on us the nature of the relation in which God stands to each one of us; and very frequently these appeals are accompanied with the assurance that the love of the human parent is but a faint reflection of the love of the Heavenly Father. What can be more touching than the appeal of the prophet Isaiah? "Can a woman forget her suckling child, that she should not have compassion on the son of her womb? Yea, they may forget, yet will not I forget thee" [Isaiah 49:15]. The parallel passage in the New Testament is this: "If ye then, being evil, know how to give good gifts to your children, how much more will your Heavenly Father give!" [cf. Luke 11:13]. But we all feel that the first and ever-during duty of a father is to endeavor to make his child righteous. A righteous father must always do this. The moment he ceases to do this, he ceases to be a righteous father. However the son transgresses, we never feel that the father's obligation to try to bring him back be dissolved. The righteous father's heart goes along with his obligation; he could not give up his son although the whole world agreed that he had done all that could be done for him, and that it was useless to try any more. And shall we not reason confidently that the righteous Heavenly Father will do exceedingly abundantly above all that the righteous earthly father can either desire or effect? But does this desire for the righteousness of his child, in the heart of the earthly father, terminate with the child's life? Although he is only the father of his body, does he not yearn after the soul of his son who has been, perhaps, cut off suddenly in the midst of sin and thoughtlessness? He does indeed yearn after his soul, and carries it on his heart a heavy burden, mourning all his life long, and wavering between hope and fear as to what his everlasting lot may be. The righteous earthly father, being only the father of the child's body, feels thus and acts thus; can we suppose that the Father of the spirits of all flesh will throw off His care for the souls of His children when they leave this world, because they have, during their stay here, resisted His efforts to make them righteous? The supposition seems monstrous and incredible and in truth could not be acquiesced in by any human being, were it not for certain false ideas concerning the justice or righteousness of God.

I believe that love and righteousness and justice in God mean exactly the same thing, namely, a desire to bring His whole moral creation into a participation of His own character and His own blessedness. He has made us capable of this, and He will not cease from using the best means for accomplishing it in us all. When I think of God making a creature of such capacities, it seems to me almost blasphemous to suppose that He will throw it from Him into everlasting darkness, because it has resisted His gracious purposes towards it for the natural period of human life. No; He who waited so long for the formation of a piece of old red sandstone will surely wait with much long-suffering for the perfecting of a human spirit.

I have found myself helped in taking hold of this hope by understanding that God really made man that he might educate him, not that He might try him. If we suppose man to be merely on his trial here, we more readily adopt the idea of a final judgment coming after the day of trial is over. But if we suppose man to be created, not to be tried, but to be educated, we cannot believe that the education is to terminate with this life, considering that there is so large a proportion of the human race who die in infancy, and that of those who survive that period there are so many who can scarcely be said to receive any education at all, and that so few — not one in a million — appear to benefit by their education. That, as there are great judgment days in the world, so there will be great judgment days in the other world, I have no doubt; but I believe they are all subservient to the grand purpose of spiritual education. We are judged in order thereby to be educated; we are not educated that we may be judged. I believe that each individual human being has been created to fill a particular place in the great body of Jesus Christ, and that a special education is needed to fit each one for his place. Whilst we are ignorant of the destined place of each, it must of course be impossible for us to understand the wonderful variety of treatment through which the great Teacher is conducting all by a right way to the right end. But He knows and does what is best and wisest; and may there not be a necessity in some cases for treatment which can only be had on the other side of the grave? And shall we in our short-sightedness consider Him debarred from any such treatment?

I cannot believe that any human being can be beyond the reach of God's grace and the sanctifying power of His Spirit. And if all are within His reach, is it possible to suppose that He will allow any to remain unsanctified? Is not the love revealed in Jesus Christ a love unlimited, unbounded, which will not leave undone anything which love could desire? It was surely nothing else than the complete and universal triumph of that love which Paul was contemplating when he cried out, "Oh the depth of the riches both of the wisdom and knowledge of God!" (Rom. xi.33).

Let me conclude now by saying that I am persuaded that this doctrine which you advocate is the only sufficient ground for an entire confidence in God, which shall, at the same time, be a righteous confidence. According to it, God created man that he might be a partaker in His own holiness as the only right and blessed state possible for him. If I truly apprehend this — if I truly apprehend that righteousness and blessedness are one and the same thing, and just the very thing I most need — I shall rejoice to know that God desires my righteousness; and if I further know that He will never cease to desire it and to insist upon it, and that all His dealings with me are for this one end, then I can have an entire confidence in Him, as desiring for me the very thing I desire for myself. I shall feel that I am perfectly safe in His hand, that I could not be so safe in any other hand; for that, as He desires the best thing for me, so He alone knows and can use the best means of accomplishing it in me. Thus I can actually adopt the sentiment of the Psalmist, and say, "Thou art my strong habitation, whereunto I may continually resort. Thou hast given commandment to save me, for Thou art my rock and fortress" [Psalm 71:3]. And I can adopt these words without any feeling of self-trust, because my confidence has no back look to myself, but rests simply on God. The greatest sinner upon earth might at once adopt these words, if he only saw that righteousness was his true and only possible blessedness, and that God would never cease from desiring this righteousness for him. I am fully persuaded that the real meaning of believing in Jesus Christ is believing in this eternal purpose of God, the purpose of making us living members of the body of His Son. And as this blessed faith helps me to love God and trust Him for myself, so it helps me to love my fellow-creatures, because it assures me that, however debased and unlovable they may be at present, yet the time is coming when they shall all be living members of Christ's body, partakers in the holiness and beauty and blessedness of their Lord.

(Hanna, pp. 422-429)

To the Rev. Paton J. Gloag, D.D. March 1858

I have looked through your works on Justification by Faith and on the Assurance of Salvation, and I venture to communicate to you some of the thoughts which they have suggested to me, persuaded that you will receive them candidly and kindly, not rejecting them unweighed because they do not altogether agree with what you have been accustomed to consider the orthodox standard.

I observe, from what you say in the beginning of the 184th page of the larger work, that you have felt the difficulty connected with the common theory, although you have got over it. You have felt the difficulty of believing that there could be anything conventional or arbitrary in God's dealing with man, in the spiritual education of him. Every thinking man must have felt it; and many, I am sure, have been compelled to reject the common theory, whether they have arrived at any other which satisfied them or not. Let me propose a solution. Does not the true rightness of man consist in an absolute submissive dependence on God as a loving Father, who is continually, by His Spirit within and His providence without, seeking to bring us into an entire conformity with His own will? Does it not consist in such a dependence as the branch has on the vine, living by the sap thence received? Does not man's wrongness consist in his following his own independent will, in acting from his own resources, in living under the power of self? Faith, confidence, dependence, is the name for man's turning from himself to God. "Trust in the Lord with all thy heart, and lean not to thine own understanding; in all thy ways acknowledge Him, and He will direct thy paths" [Proverbs 3:6]. This faith is man's right condition, and it is the righteousness of Christ, as the sap in the branch is the sap from the vine. When I entirely trust in another, so as to surrender myself to his guidance, the righteousness of that other is communicated to me. This is, I believe, the *dikaiosune* which is on all men whether they believe it or not, the manifestation of the loving purpose of God toward them in Jesus Christ, but which does not become *dikaiosune*, righteousness, until it is received by faith, the spiritual apprehension.

I believe that the Son of God, the eternal Word, is the original foundation and ground of man's being; that man is in the image of God because created in Him who is the express image of the Father; that man's acting as if he were his own or had anything of his own, and not as existing in Christ, is his fall and unrighteousness; but that does not and cannot get him off the deep original ground of his being. I believe that as Christ is the ground of man's being, and is actually in every man as the supplier of spiritual life, so He is also the Head of man, of the whole race of man, acting for the race, not at all as their substitute, but as their Head and root; doing things, not instead of them, but for them, as the root does things for the branches.

I have no belief in the forensic theory, which seems to me founded on a mistaken conception of God's relation to man. It supposes that God's chief relation to man is that of a judge, and that the relations of Father and teacher must suit themselves to it, in subordination to it; whereas I am convinced that it is just the contrary. The forensic system supposes that God made men that he may afterwards judge them; I believe that he judges them that He may teach them, so that his judgments are instructions. I believe that God created man that He might instruct him into a conformity with His own character. This view of the purpose of God in man's creation makes an important change in our feelings with regard to the Law. Whilst I regard God as my Judge, the law is an object of fear, and the higher its standard the greater is that fear; whereas if I regard God as my Fatherly teacher, seeking to make me a partaker of His blessedness by making me partaker in His holiness, I am delighted with the contemplation of the high standard to which He is using means to elevate me, and instead of shunning this searching eye, I desire to expose myself to it, knowing that it is the eye not of a taskmaster who is seeking occasion against me, but the eye of a loving spiritual physician who is searching into my disease in order to cure it. The 139th Psalm is a beautiful exemplification of the effect of this apprehension of God and His purpose towards us. David, conscious of much sin and pollution, welcomes the gaze of God, assured that His object is to lead him in the way everlasting. When I am sure that God's one and sole purpose towards me is to deliver me from everything that can separate me from Himself and His eternal blessedness, I can lay myself down with absolute security in His hand, receiving His discipline in whatever form it comes, saying "Search me, O Lord, and know my heart; try me and know my ways, and lead me in the way everlasting" [Psalm 139:23-24].

I believe that this state of spiritual being is the true justification by faith and the true assurance of salvation, and that these can never be produced by any feeling that we have complied with any condition, either faith or obedience (which, in fact, come to the same thing), but that they can only be produced by seeing in the character of God that thorough fatherliness on which we can place a perfect reliance, and by discovering that His purpose for us is just what we most desire for ourselves. I find it most sweet when I can thus rest on the eternal love of my Father's heart, sweeter far than to rest on any thought (most dubious at best) that I have fulfilled a prescribed condition of either faith or obedience, and sweeter also than to rest on the idea of a legal transaction by which my debt to God has been paid. I wish to owe Him all, to owe Him a debt of love which never can be paid. If I believed in the forensic theory I should feel that in coming to it from the 139th Psalm I had come from a higher, holier ground to a lower and less holy, which I am sure is impossible in the progress of divine revelation.

Jesus is the revealer of the Father, and His doings have their chief value in discovering to us the everlasting Fountain out of which they flowed. It seems to me that at every step of His earthly course we should hear Him saying, "He that hath seen me hath seen the Father" [John 14:9]; and what were all these steps but a varied manifestation of the desire to seek and save the lost? What were they but varied expressions of sympathy for man pressed down by sin and sorrow? So the miraculous cures are less considered by the evangelists as acts of power than as acts of compassion, tokens of sympathy (Matt. viii.17). And thus He revealed the Father. And in that touching invitation which concludes the 11th chapter of the same book the true meaning of the whole passage is missed unless we see it in its connection with the last clause of the 27th verse, "Neither knoweth any man the Father save the Son, and he to whomsoever the Son will reveal him;" and now come unto me, for I am the Son ready to reveal the Father, and so to give you rest.

But I must stop, for I shall be writing you a book and not a letter if I go on. One thing, however, I should be sorry to omit, which is, that the forensic theory has a direct tendency to make men think that salvation consists in the removal of a penalty instead of a deliverance from sin. I am persuaded that it has had that effect on the minds of our population very universally.

And now, dear sir, hoping and trusting that you will interpret kindly both what I have written and my purpose in writing, I subscribe myself your obedient servant.

T. Erskine

P.S. — When I use the phrase "forensic theory," I mean that theory of the work of Christ which contains the idea that God is compelled by His own essential justice to punish sin, and to punish it as an infinite offence because it is committed against His own infinite excellence, and that in order to evade this necessity, which would involve the perdition of the whole race, He has had recourse to substitutional imputation. It seems to me that there is a mistake at the very foundation of all this. I do not believe that justice is, or can be, satisfied with punishment. I believe that the justice of God is the righteousness of God, and that His righteousness requires righteousness in man, and can be satisfied with nothing else, and that punishment is God's protest that he is not satisfied. But it is evident that if this be so the judicial office is incomplete in itself, and must be subordinate to the teaching office, so that the condemnation of wrong may minister to the inculcation and acquisition of right.

I can see many causes for the marked unfruitfulness of religious instruction amongst us, but I am persuaded that the chief are that the judicial character of God is made to swallow up and conceal His paternal character; that thus Christ is viewed as a refuge from the Father instead of the way to Him, and that the Law is represented as a standard by which we are to be tried and condemned, instead of a standard to which it is the purpose of God to raise and draw us up. I believe that the true assurance of salvation is unattainable where such thoughts exist and prevail. Finally, I believe that we are all called and elected to eternal life, but that we may frustrate the counsel of God, and that therefore we are exhorted to make our calling and election sure, not to make ourselves sure that we are called and elected, but to make our undoubted calling and election *bebaian*, firm, solid ...

Farewell, dear sir; I trust that you will not think me either presumptuous or officious in thus writing to you.

T. Erskine

(Hanna, pp. 391–397)

I. THE WORKS OF THOMAS ERSKINE

Remarks on the Internal Evidence for the Truth of Revealed Religion. Edinburgh: Waugh & Innes, 1820. (Edition consulted: Third American from the Fifth Enlarged Edinburgh Edition. Andover, MA: Warren F. Draper, 1860.) German translation: *Bemerkungen über die innern Grunde der Wahrheit der geoffenbaren Religion.* Leipzig, 1825. French translation: *Réflexions sur l'évidence intrinsèque de la vérité du christianisme.* Paris, 1822.

The Works of John Gambold, A.M., with an Introductory Essay, by Thomas Erskine, Esq. Advocate. Glasgow: Chalmers & Collins, 1822.

An Essay on Faith. Edinburgh: Waugh & Innes, 1822. (Edition consulted: Second American Edition. Portsmouth, NH: T.H. Miller, 1826.) French translation: *Essai sur la foi.* Paris, 1826.

Introductory Essay to The Saints' Everlasting Rest by the Rev. Richard Baxter. Glasgow: Collins Select Christian Authors, 1824. (Edition consulted: Boston: Perkins & Marvin, 1833.)

Letters of the Rev. Samuel Rutherford, Late Professor of Divinity at St. Andrews. With an Introductory Essay by Thomas Erskine, Esq. Advocate. Glasgow: Chalmers and Collins, 1825. (Also appended to the 10th edition of *Remarks on the Internal Evidence*, &c. Edinburgh, 1878.)

The Unconditional Freeness of the Gospel. Edinburgh: Waugh & Innes, 1828. (Edition consulted: New Edition. Edinburgh: David Doublas, 1879.) French translation: (1) *Première essai sur la gratuité de l'Evangile.* Bordeaux: Lanefranque aine, 1833. (2) *Gratuité absolue de l'Evangile. Deuxième essai.* Valence: M. Aurel Frères, 1839. (3) *Indulgence plenière sans conditions, ou gratuité absolue de l'Evangile.* Valence: M. Aurel Frères, 1839.

The Gifts of the Spirit. Greenock: R.B. Luck, 1830.

Extracts of Letters to a Christian Friend by a Lady, with an Introductory Essay by Thomas Erskine, Esq. Advocate. Greenock: R.B. Luck, 1830. (Published later, in a slightly shorter version, as *True and False Religion, by the late Thomas Erskine of Linlathen.* London: Hamilton, Adams, and Co., 1874.

The Brazen Serpent, or Life Coming through Death. Edinburgh: Waugh & Innes, 1831. (Edition consulted: Third Edition. Edinburgh: David Douglas, 1879.)

The Doctrine of Election and its Connection with the General Tenor of Christianity, Illustrated from many Parts of Scripture and especially from the Epistle to the Romans. London: James Duncan, 1837.

The Spiritual Order and Other Papers. Selected from the Manuscripts of the late Thomas Erskine of Linlathen. Edinburgh: Edmonston & Douglas, 1871. (The third essay in this collection was published separately and in a shorter version as *The Purpose of God in the Creation of Man.* Edinburgh: Edmonston & Douglas, 1870.)

William Hanna (ed.) *Letters of Thomas Erskine of Linlathen.* (2 vols.) Edinburgh: David Douglas, 1877. (Edition consulted: Third Edition. Edinburgh: David Douglas, 1878.)

Alexander Ewing (ed.). *Present-Day Papers on Prominent Questions in Theology.* Third Series. London: Daldy, Isbister & Co., 1878. (Part 1: Letters of Thomas Erskine of Linlathen. Part 4: *Some Further Letters of Thomas Erskine of Linlathen.* Part 6: *The Relation of Knowledge to Salvation,* by the Editor, with Letters from the Archbishop of Canterbury, Bishop Thirwall, the Rev. Dr. McLeod Campbell, and Mr. Erskine. Part 7: *Reconciliation,* by the Editor. With Letters from the Rev. Dr. McLeod Campbell, the Rev. F.D. Maurice, and Mr. Erskine.)

_____. *The Internal Word, or Light Becoming Life. A Short Guide to the Rule of Faith and of Life. Being an Abridgement of the Concluding Portion of Mr. Erskine's Volume on the Doctrine of Election.* Edinburgh: Edmonston and Douglas, 1865.

Francis Russell (ed). *The Fatherhood of God Revealed in Christ, the Comfort and Hope of Man. A Lesson From "The Letters" of Thomas Erskine of Linlathen.* Edinburgh: David Douglas, 1888.

Henry F. Henderson (ed.) *Erskine of Linlathen: Selections and Biography.* Edinburgh and London: Oliphant Anderson & Ferrier, 1899.

W. Fraser Mitchell (ed.) *The Purpose of Life. Selections Mainly from the Correspondence of Erskine of Linlathen.* London: The Epworth Press, 1945.

II. SUPLEMENTARY BIBLIOGRAPHY

"Anglicanus." *View of the Character, Position, and Prospects of the Edinburgh Bible Society. In Seven Letters.* Edinburgh, 1827.

_____. *Universal Redemption, a Truth according to the Scriptures, Defended from the Misrepresentations and Calumnies contained in a Late Pamphlet entitled "The Gareloch Heresy Tried," in a Letter Addressed to the Rev. Robert Burns, D.D., Author of the Aforesaid Pamphlet.* Glasgow: W. Collins, &c., 1830.

Anonymous. *Candour; or an Impartial Examination of the Row Heresy: with Hints to the General Assembly on the Treatment of Controversies.* Glasgow: W.R. McPhun, 1831.

_____. *Critical Remarks on the Everlasting Gospel; A Sermon preached in the Floating Chapel at Greenock, by the Rev. J.M. Campbell, Minister of Row, Dumbartonshire.* Edinburgh: R.B. Luck, 1830.

_____. *An Examination and Refutation of the Unscriptural Principles and Sentiments advocated by Mr. Erskine in his Preface [sic] to "Extracts of Letters to a Christian Friend; by a Lady."* Edinburgh: J. & D. Collie, 1830.

_____. *A Letter to a Friend, on Universal Pardon, as advanced by Thomas Erskine, Esq., and Others.* Dundee: James Adam, 1830.

_____. "The Letters of Thomas Erskine" [= review of Hanna (ed.), Vol. 1], *The Spectator*, 23 June 1877, pp. 793-4.

_____. "The Letters of Thomas Erskine" [= review of Hanna (ed.), Vol. 2], *The Spectator*, 29 Dec. 1877, pp. 1661-2.

_____. "Mr. Erskine's Posthumous Fragments [= review of *The Spiritual Order*], *The Spectator*, 24 June 1871, pp. 768-70.

_____. *The Port Glasgow Miracles, on a Publication entitled: The Gifts of the Spirit, by Thomas Erskine, Esqr. Advocate.* Hamburgh: Hartwick & Müller, 1830.

_____. Review of 'Anglicanus': *View of the Character, Position, and Prospects of the Edinburgh Bible Society. Edinburgh Christian Instructor*, Vol. 27, No. 1 (Jan., 1828), pp. 1-85.

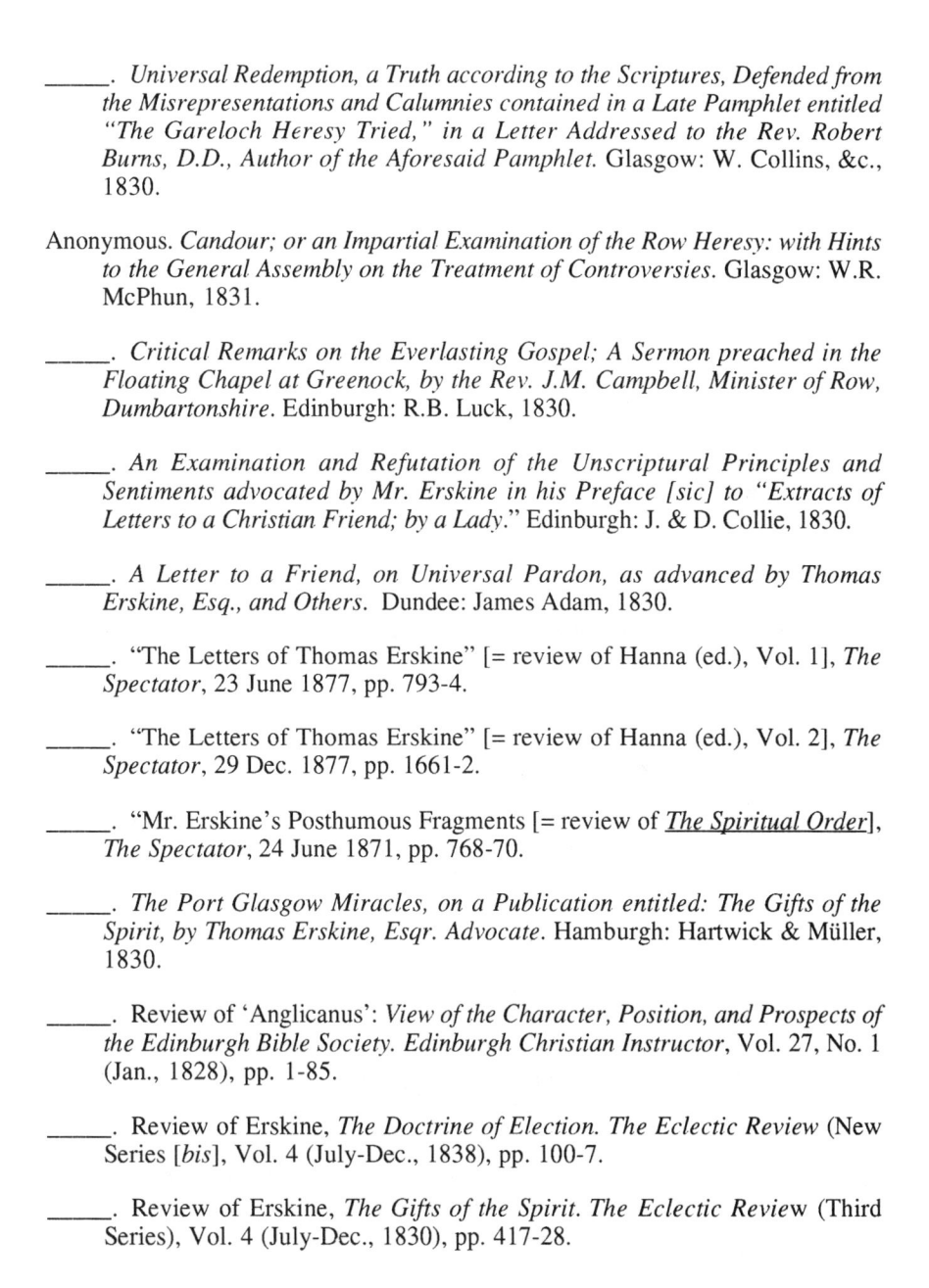

_____. Review of Erskine, *The Doctrine of Election. The Eclectic Review* (New Series [*bis*], Vol. 4 (July-Dec., 1838), pp. 100-7.

_____. Review of Erskine, *The Gifts of the Spirit. The Eclectic Review* (Third Series), Vol. 4 (July-Dec., 1830), pp. 417-28.

_____. Review of Erskine, *Remarks on the Internal Evidence for the Truth of Revealed Religion*. The Eclectic Review (New Series), vol. 16 (July-Dec., 1821), pp. 180-5.

_____. Review of Erskine, *The Unconditional Freeness of the Gospel*. The British Critic, Quarterly Theological Review, and Ecclesiastical Record, Vol. 5 (1829), pp. 54-80.

_____. Review of G.S. Faber, *The Primitive Doctrine of Election*, and of Erskine, *The Doctrine of Election*. The British Critic and Quarterly Review, Vol. 23 (1838), pp. 299-328.

_____. Review of Publications in the Row Heresy. *Edinburgh Christian Instructor*, Vol. 29, No. 4 (May, 1830), pp. 332-52.

_____. Review of several works relating to the Row Heresy, including Erskine's "Introductory Essay" to *Extracts of Letters to a Christian Friend, by a Lady*. The Eclectic Review (Third Series), Vol. 4 (July-Dec., 1830), pp. 61-77.

_____. Review of "A Vindication of the 'Religion of the Land' &c. by A. Robertson," *Edinburgh Christian Instructor*, Vol. 29, No. 7 (July, 1830), pp. 520-4.

_____. *Thoughts on the Doctrine of Assurance. A Letter to a Friend. By a Member of the Church of Scotland*. Glasgow: Geo. Gallie, 1828.

M. Charles Bell. *Calvin and Scottish Theology: The Doctrine of Assurance*. Edinburgh: The Handsel Press, 1985.

Eugene Garrett Bewkes. *Legacy of a Christian Mind: John M'Leod Campbell, Eminent Contributor to Theological Thought*. Philadelphia: The Judson Press, 1937.

Olive J. Brose. *Frederick Denison Maurice: Rebellious Conformist*. Athens: Ohio University Press, 1971.

Peter Brotherston. *A Brief View of Faith; in which the Saving Belief of the Gospel is Distinguished from Antinomian Confidence*. Edinburgh: William Whyte, 1828.

John Brown (ed.). *Letters of Dr. John Brown with Letters from Ruskin, Thackeray, and Others, Edited by his Son and D.W. Forrest, D.D., with Biographical Introductions by Elizabeth T. McLaren*. London: Adam & Charles Black, 1907.

James Bryce. *Ten Years of the Church of Scotland from 1833 to 1843 with Historical Retrospect from 1560* (2 vols.). Edinburgh and London: William Blackwood and Sons, 1850.

[James Buchanan] *A Letter to Thomas Erskine, Esq. Advocate. Containing Remarks on His Late Work entitled "The Unconditional Freeness of the Gospel," by a Minister of the Church of Scotland.* Edinburgh: John Lindsay, 1828.

Robert Burns. *The Church Revived Without the Aid of Unknown Tongues. A Sermon.* London: A. Douglas, 1831.

_____. *The Gairloch Heresy Tried; in a Letter to the Rev. John M. Campbell, of Row; and a Sermon preached at Helensburgh and at Port-Glasgow.* Paisley: Alex. Gardner, 1830.

_____. *Reply to a Lay Member of the Church of Scotland; with a Note for the Reverend James Russel ... by the Author of the Gareloch Heresy Tried.* Paisley: Alex. Gardner, 1830.

W.R. Caird, *A Letter to the Rev. R.H. Story, Rosneath, Respecting Certain Misstatements Contained in his Memoir of the Late Rev. R. Story.* Edinburgh: Thomas Lauir, 1863.

John McLeod Campbell. *Reminiscences and Reflections Referring to His Early Ministry in the Parish of Row, 1825-1831. Edited, with an Introductory Narrative, by his Son, Donald Campbell, M.A.* London: Macmillan and Co., 1873.

Thomas Carlyle. *Letters of Thomas Carlyle to his Youngest Sister. Edited with an Introductory Essay by Charles Townsend Copeland.* London: Chapman and Hall, 1899.

[Thomas Carlyle] *Letter to the Rev. Robert Burns, D.D., F.S.A., and the Rev. William Hamilton, D.D., occasioned by their Late Publications entitled "The Gairloch Heresy Tried," and "Remarks on Certain Opinions Recently Propagated, Respecting Universal Redemption," &c. by a Lay Member of the Church of Scotland.* Greenock: R.B. Lusk, 1830. (NB. This is not Thomas Carlyle, the celebrated author, but the advocate who defended Mr. Campbell at his heresy trial and who subsequently became an influential member of the Irvingite Church.

_____. *Protestant Truths and Popish Errors: A Letter to the Author of "The Gareloch Heresy Tried," occasioned by His Reply to the Lay Member of the*

Church of Scotland: with a Postscript Addressed to the Rev. Dr. Hamilton, Strathblane. Greenock: R.B. Lusk, 1830.

Moncure Daniel Conway. *Autobiography—Memories and Experiences* (2 vols.). Boston: Houghton, Mifflin, 1904.

Edward Craig. *A Letter to Thomas Erskine, Esq. in Reply to his Recent Pamphlet in Vindication of the West Country Miracles.* Edinburgh: William Oliphant, 1830.

David Davidson. *A Sermon, on Acts x.43; in which the Doctrine of Universal Pardon is Considered and Refuted.* Dundee: Jas. Chalmers, 1830.

Philip Devinish. "Divinity and Dipolarity: Thomas Erskine and Charles Hartshorne on What Makes God 'God'," *Journal of Religion*, 62 (1982), pp. 335-58.

Andrew L. Drummond and James Bulloch. *The Church in Victorian Scotland.* Edinburgh: The Saint Andrew Press, 1975.

_____. *The Scottish Church 1688-1843.* Edinburgh: The Saint Andrew Press, 1973.

Alexander Duncan. *A Sermon on the Various Forms of Universalism, with an Appendix on Assurance.* Glasgow: M. Lochhead, 1831.

Alexander Ewing. *An Address to the Younger Clergy and Laity on the Present State of Religion, &c.* London: Longman, Green &c., 1865.

George S. Faber. *The Primitive Doctrine of Election; or an Historical Inquiry into the Ideality and Causation of Scriptural Election, as Received and Maintained in the Primitive Church of Christ.* London: Wm. Crofts, 1836.

Duncan Finlayson. "Aspects of the Life and Influence of Thomas Erskine of Linlathen, 1788-1870," *Records of Scottish Church History Review*, Vol. 20, Part 1 (1978), pp. 31-45.

Robert S. Franks. *The Work of Christ: A Historical Study of Christian Doctrine.* London: Th. Nelson and Sons, 1962 (= reprint of the 1918 edition entitled *A History of the Doctrine of the Work of Christ*).

Joseph Gilbert. *The Christian Atonement; its Basis, Nature, and Bearings: or, the Principle of Substitution Illustrated as Applied in the Redemption of Man.* London: Wm. Bell, 1836.

Frederick Goldie. *A Short History of the Episcopal Church in Scotland*. London: S.P.C.K., 1951.

Steve Gowler. "No Second-hand Religion: Thomas Erskine's Critique of Religious Authorities," *Church History*, 54 (1985), pp. 202-14.

Henry Grey. *Remarks Relative to his Connection with the Letters of Anglicanus*. Edinburgh: Brown & Wardlay, 1828.

George Grub. *An Ecclesiastical History of Scotland* (4 vols.). Edinburgh: Edmonston & Douglas, 1861.

J.A. Haldane. *Observations of Universal Pardon, the Extent of the Atonement, and Personal Assurance of Salvation*. Edinburgh: W. Whyte & Co., 1831.

Robert Haldane. *Exposure of the Rev. Henry Grey's Personal Misrepresentations, Doctrinal Heresies, and Important Mistatements [sic] respecting the Bible Society, as contained in the Letters of Anglicanus*. Edinburgh: William Whyte & Co., 1828.

William Hamilton. *Remarks on Certain Opinions Propagated, Respecting Universal Redemption, &c*. Glasgow: Maurice Ogle, 1830.

William Hanna. *Memoirs of the Life and Writings of Thomas Chalmers, D.D., LL.D*. New York: Harper and Brothers, 1850-52.

Henry F. Henderson. *The Religious Controversies of Scotland*. Edinburgh: T. & T. Clark, 1905.

Florence Hingham. *Frederick Denison Maurice*. London: SCM, 1947.

John Howe. *The Carnality of Religious Contention*. London: Th. Parkhurst, 1693 and Edinburgh, 1846.

Richard H. Hutton. "The Incarnation and Principles of Evidence, with a Letter to the Writer, by the Rev. F. D. Maurice," *Tracts for Priests and People*, No. XIV. London: Macmillan and Co., 1862.

Soame Jenyns. *A View of the Internal Evidence for the Christian Religion* (tenth ed.). Edinburgh: Mundell & Son, 1798.

Fred Kaplan. *Thomas Carlyle: A Biography*. Ithaca: Cornell University Press, 1983.

William Angus Knight. *Principal Shairp and His Friends*. London: John Murray, 1888.

J. Leslie. *The "Christian Instructor" Instructed; or Important Observations on the "Irving and Row Heresies," Contained in a Letter Addressed to Dr. A. Thomson. Also, a Letter to J.A. Haldane, Esq*. Edinburgh (privately printed), 1830.

Varnum Lincoln. "Thomas Erskine of Linlathen, His Life, Writings, and Theology," *Universalist Quarterly and General Review* (1880), pp. 149-63.

John B. Logan, "Thomas Erskine of Linlathen: Lay Theologian of the 'Inner Light'," *Scottish Journal of Theology*, 37 (1984), pp. 202-14.

_____. *The Religious Thought of Thomas Erskine of Linlathen*. New York: Union Theological Seminary Master's Thesis, 1931.

Agnes Maule Machar, "Leaders of Widening Religious Thought and Life," *Andover Review*, 14 (1890), pp. 464-79, 588-609.

Jean Baptiste Massillon. *A Sermon Preached on the Third Monday of Lent, on the Small Number of the Elect*. Edinburgh: Archibald Constable, 1817.

David Maclagen. *St. George's, Edinburgh. A History of St. George's Church 1814 to 1843 and of St. George's Free Church 1843 to 1873*. London: T. Nelson & Sons, 1876.

John Macleod. *Scottish Theology in Relation to Church History since the Reformation*. Edinburgh: The Banner of Truth Trust, 1943.

J. Malcolm. *The Parish of Monifieth in Ancient and Modern Times with a History of the Landed Estates and Lives of Eminent Men*. Edinburgh and London: William Green & Sons, 1910.

Frederick Maurice. *The Life of Frederick Denison Maurice Chiefly Told in His Own Letters* (2 vols.). New York: Charles Scribner's Sons, 1884.

Frederick Denison Maurice. "Dedication to Thomas Erskine, Esq., of Linlathen," in *The Prophets and Kings of the Old Testament*, Fifth Edition, (London: Macmillan and Co., 1894), pp. v-xii.

_____. *The Gospel of John. A Series of Discourses*. Second Edition. London: Macmillan, 1894.

Frank Maudlin McClain. *Maurice: Man and Moralist.* London: S.P.C.K., 1972.

Adam Milroy. "The Doctrine of the Church of Scotland," in Robert H. Story (ed.), *The Church of Scotland, Past and Present: Its History, Its Relation to the Law and State, Its Doctrine, Ritual, Discipline, and Patrimony.* (London: Wm. Mackenzie, 1895), Vol. 4, pp. 133-302.

James Bowling Mozley. "Maurice's Theological Essays," in *Essays Historical and Theological*, Vol. 2 (New York: E.P. Dutton and Company, 1878), pp. 255-309. (Originally published in the *Christian Remembrancer* of January, 1854.)

John Henry Newman. "On the Introduction of Rationalistic Principles into Religion," *Tracts for the Times*, No. 73. London: Rivington, 1836.

"No Unitarian." "Letter to the Editor," *Edinburgh Christian Instructor*, Vol. 29, No. 6 (June, 1830), pp. 409-10.

Margaret O.W. Oliphant. *A Memoir of the Life of John Tulloch, D.D., LL.D.* Second Edition. Edinburgh and London: Wm. Blackwood & Sons, 1888.

Archibald Paterson. *Passages of Scripture and Remarks on the Universal Pardon from the First Condemnation; with an Appendix containing Particular Answers to the Several Texts contained in "A Treatise upon the Forgiveness of Sins in Opposition to the Doctrine of Universal Pardon," by the Rev. John Smith [Smyth], A.M. Minister of St. George's Glasgow.* Second Edition. Glasgow (privately printed), 1830.

Otto Pfleiderer. *The Development of Theology in Germany since Kant and its Progress in Great Britain since 1825.* (Translated by J.F. Smith.) London; Swan Sonneschein & Co., 1890.

"Priest Evangelist" [Edward Craig]. *Epistle on the Final Salvation of all Mankind from Sin, to the Angel of the "Holy Catholic Apostolic Church in Glasgow," with a Letter to the Author, from Thos. Erskine, Esq., Advocate.* Second Edition. Glasgow: George Gallie, 1863.

Bernard M.G. Reardon. *From Coleridge to Gore: A Century of Religious Thought in Britain.* London: Longman, 1871.

Robert A. Reid. *The Influence, Direct and Indirect, of the Writings of Erskine of Linlathen on Religious Thought in Scotland.* Thesis, New College, Edinburgh, 1930.

James H. Rigg. *Modern Anglican Theology: Chapters on Coleridge, Hare, Maurice, Kingsley, and Jowett, and on the Doctrine of Sacrifice and Atonement.* Second Edition. London: A. Heylin, 1859.

Archibald Robertson. *A Vindication of "The Religion of the Land" from Misrepresentations and an Exposure of the Absurd Pretensions of the Gareloch Enthusiasts. In a Letter to Thomas Erskine, Esq., Advocate.* Edinburgh: William Whyte & Co., 1830.

Geoffrey Rowell. *Hell and the Victorians.* Oxford: Clarendon Press, 1974.

David Russel. *The Way of Salvation, A Discourse, &c., Second Edition, with Additional Notes and Illustrations; Containing Remarks on the Doctrine of Universal Pardon.* Dundee: Jas. Chalmers, 1830.

Richard H. Shepherd and Charles W. Williamson (ed.). *Memoirs of the Life and Writings of Thomas Carlyle, with Personal Reminiscences, &c.* (2 vols.). London: W.H. Allen & Co., 1881.

Donald C. Smith. *Passive Obedience and Prophetic Protest: Social Criticism in the Scottish Church 1830-1945.* New York: P. Lang, 1987.

John Smyth. "Internal Evidence of Christianity," in *Lectures on the Evidence of Revealed Religion, by Ministers of the Established Church in Glasgow.* (Glasgow: Wm. Collins, 1838), pp. 338-73.

_____. *A Treatise on the Forgiveness of Sins as the Privilege of the Redeemed; in Opposition to the Doctrine of Universal Pardon.* Glasgow: Th. Ogilvie, 1830.

William Stephen. *History of the Scottish Church* (2 vols.). Edinburgh: David Douglas, 1896.

Vernon F. Storr. *The Development of English Theology in the Nineteenth Century, 1800-1860.* London: Longmans, Green & Co., 1913.

Robert H. Story. *The Apostolic Ministry in the Scottish Church.* Edinburgh and London: William Blackwood and Sons, 1897.

_____. *Memoir of the Life of the Rev. Robert Story.* Cambridge: Macmillan and Co., 1862.

_____. *The Risen Christ: A Sermon Preached in Rosneath on the Lord's Day after the Death of John McLeod Campbell, D.D.* Glasgow: James Maclehose, 1872.

Andrew Thomson. *The Doctrine of Universal Pardon Considered and Refuted in a Series of Sermons, with Notes, Critical and Expository.* Edinburgh: William Whyte and Co., 1830.

_____. "Review of *The Gairloch Heresy Tried*, &c. by the Rev. Rob. Burns," *Edinburgh Christian Instructor*, Vol. 29, No. 2 (Feb., 1830), pp. 102ff.

_____. "Review of *The Unconditional Freeness of the Gospel, in Three Essays.* By Thomas Erskine," *Edinburgh Christian Instructor*, Vol. 27, No. 6 (June, 1828), pp. 410-27.

John Tulloch. *Movements of Religious Thought in Britain during the Nineteenth Century.* New York: Humanities Press, 1971 (reprint of 1885 edition).

James Ussher. *A Letter concerning the Death and Satisfaction of Christ. Written March 3, 1617, by the Most Rev. James Ussher, D.D. Archbishop of Armagh, and Primate of all Ireland. To which is added, His Grace's Answer to some Exceptions Taken Against the Above Letter.* Edinburgh: William Oliphant, 1831.

D.J. Vaughn. "Scottish Influences on English Theological Thought," *The Contemporary Review*, Vol. 32 (1878), pp. 457-73.

Alec R. Vidler. "Thomas Erskine," in *F.D. Maurice and Company: Nineteenth Century Studies.* (London: SCM, 1966), pp. 242-9.

James Walker. *The Theology and Theologians of Scotland.* Edinburgh: T. & T. Clark, 1888.

Norman L. Walker. *Robert Buchanan, D.D. An Ecclesiastical Biography.* London: Thomas Nelson and Sons, 1877.

Ralph Wardlaw. *Discourses on the Nature and Extent of the Atonement of Christ.* Glasgow: James Maclehose, 1843.

_____. *Two Essays: On the Assurance of Faith; On the Extent of the Atonement and Universal Pardon.* Glasgow, 1830.

Jean L. Watson. *Life of Andrew Thomson, D.D., Minister of St. George's Parish, Edinburgh.* Edinburgh: James Gemmell, 1882.

Julia Wedgwood. "Thomas Erskine of Linlathen," in *Nineteenth Century Teachers and Other Essays* (London: Hodder & Stoughton, 1909), pp. 63-78.

(Originally published in *The Contemporary Review*, Vol. 14 [May, 1870], pp. 260-72.)

The Whole Proceedings before the Presbytery of Dumbarton, and the Synod of Glasgow and Ayr, in the Case of the Rev. John McLeod Campbell, Minister of Row. Including the Libel, Answers to the Libel, Evidence, and Speeches. Greenock: R.B. Lusk, 1831.

William Howie Wylie. *Thomas Carlyle: The Man and His Books*. London: Marshall Japp and Company, 1881.